D1799987

Sal

Happy Christmas
& New Year —
hope this will
bring happy
memories when
you're back in
the U.K.

With our best
love —

Mike Margie Sam.

Christmas 1976.

QUEENSLAND SKETCHBOOK

THE SKETCHBOOK SERIES

QUEENSLAND SKETCHBOOK

Drawings by
UNK WHITE
KEVIN JOPSON
AINSLIE ROBERTS

Text by
PETER NEWELL

RIGBY

This edition first published in 1976 by Rigby Limited
"Brisbane" copyright © Peter Newell and Unk White 1967;
"Gold Coast and Green Mountains" copyright © Peter
Newell and Kevin Jopson 1969; "Tropical Queensland"
copyright © Ainslie Roberts and Peter Newell 1971;
"Darling Downs" copyright © Kevin Jopson and Peter Newell
1972.

ISBN 0 7270 0254 6
All rights reserved
Wholly designed and set up in Australia
Printed in Hong Kong

CONTENTS

BRISBANE

Drawings by
UNK WHITE

Text by
PETER NEWELL

CONTENTS

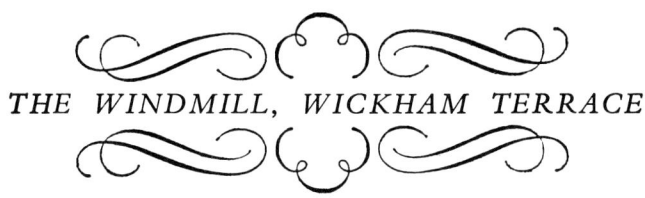

THE WINDMILL, WICKHAM TERRACE

It was the highest part of Spring Hill then known as Windmill Hill, overlooking the Brisbane township that was selected as the most suitable site for this picturesque old landmark. The mill, originally intended to grind maize for the penal settlement, was built in 1829 of sandstone blocks hewn, transported, and laid by convicts. However, when the timber sails and machinery were installed, it was found that it would not work under any circumstances.

So, when Mr Andrew Petrie was appointed the Moreton Bay settlement's overseer of works in 1837, his first task was to get the mill into operation. But, do what he would, it was never a success, and a treadmill requiring the energy of twenty-six convicts under punishment was substituted.

A Quaker visitor to the colony was horrified at the sight. On his return to London he wrote, "I am told the steps of the wheels are sometimes literally wet with the sweat that drops from the partially naked men . . . the wheel performs 160 revolutions before each man's turn of rest comes, which, multiplied by 24, the number of steps in the wheel, gives 3,840 times each man must lift his feet in continued succession. I regret that we heard the officer swearing at the men and using very improper and exasperating language."

The useless sails of the mill served as a gallows for the public hanging of two Aborigines. The execution was enthusiastically witnessed by a large mob of Aborigines, who regarded the spectacle as an entertainment rather than a grim warning!

In 1849 rumours that the mill was to be demolished led to a public outcry, and finally only the sails and domed roof were removed. After repairs it became the Government Signal Flag Station and later formed part of the Queensland Museum. It is now preserved as a tourist attraction.

NEWSTEAD HOUSE

Newstead House, Brisbane's oldest and most historical residence, built in 1846 for Patrick Leslie of Darling Downs fame, still serenely occupies the knoll which is the remaining portion of the original purchase (17 acres for £17. 10. 0), overlooking the confluence of the Brisbane River and Breakfast Creek.

Between 1847 and 1859 it was the residence of Patrick Leslie's brother-in-law, Captain John Clements Wickham, R.N., who as Government Resident for New South Wales was "charged with the general interest of government within Moreton Bay and to be representative of the Governor within its limits."

The original construction was carried out, if not by convicts, then by ticket-of-leave men. The magnificent Johnstone River fig tree in the forecourt was large even in Captain Wickham's day. Although early records describe the house as being two-storeyed, the "cottage" purchased by Captain Wickham was too small for his official entertainments, so extra rooms were added at each end. Newstead House, the unofficial Government House, became the social centre for the infant Brisbane Town, and armed guards patrolled the grounds on ball nights to discourage marauding Aborigines.

After the proclamation of the new colony of Queensland in 1859 the popular Captain Wickham's jurisdiction over Moreton Bay ended. He returned to England soon after and George Harris, a merchant and member of the Upper House, became the next inhabitant of Newstead House.

After changing hands several times, the property was acquired by the Brisbane City Council in 1918, and is now a historical museum and home of the Royal Historical Society of Queensland. The grounds are a public park.

13

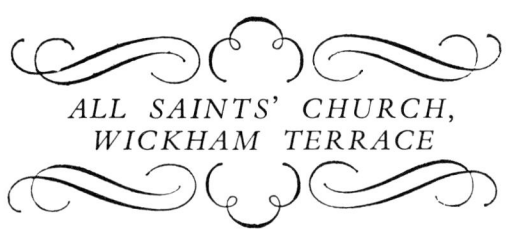

ALL SAINTS' CHURCH, WICKHAM TERRACE

In 1856, land was granted on Windmill Hill for the establishment of a church to serve the infant colony and the residents of the then fashionable suburb rapidly developing on the high land overlooking the future city.

The original stone church, familiarly called the Brisbane Tabernacle, with pews for 400, welcomed its first worshippers in 1862. By 1869 it was already too small and was reconstructed to the design of architect R. G. Suter. The old Tabernacle had been built of squared blocks of pink "porphyry" from the near-by Windsor quarries, and these were all carefully re-used, so that their present mellowness testifies to more than a century's weathering. It was at this stage that the name All Saints' Church was adopted.

A city has now grown up around its walls. When Wickham Terrace, which became Brisbane's medical district, and Ann Street were laid out, the church, set among large trees, occupied the triangular site at their junction.

The members of the congregation were greatly perturbed when they realized that a tunnel of the railway line linking Brisbane with the Valley, to be built in 1887, would pass under their church. However, the worry was needless—the sturdy 20-inch thick stone walls survived the shocks of the blasting carried out underneath their foundations.

The organ, built in 1873, was originally in old St John's procathedral in George Street. The fine stained glass windows, a gift of the Rev. T. Jones and his family in 1870. are probably the oldest in Queensland.

To mark the first centenary of All Saints', a freestanding sculpture of Christ accepting the Cross, by Andor Meszaros, was erected in the western courtyard.

15

THE DEANERY

Dr William Hobbs arrived in Brisbane in 1849 as a passenger in one of the Reverend Dr Dunmore Lang's shiploads of "worthy mechanics and virtuous migrants." Within five years he was sufficiently established to commission Andrew Petrie, that man of remarkable capacity and energy, to design and build his fine two-storey house on a knoll overlooking the river where it winds around Kangaroo Point. Adelaide House was the name he chose for his home.

In 1859, for the princely rental of £350 per year, it became the temporary Government House, in which the first Governor, Sir George Ferguson Bowen, lived while his official residence on the Domain was being built.

It was from the first-floor balcony that the new colony of Queensland was proclaimed in the presence of the Governor, on Separation Day, 10 December 1859.

When Governor Bowen took up residence in the new Government House, the Hobbs family moved back to Adelaide House. Sometime later, excavations for the Adelaide Street extension were started, and to the doctor's wrath, the zealous workmen completely destroyed his garden, which meant that the house was left standing perilously close to the steep cutting. Without the garden the house had little attraction for the Hobbs family, and they soon left.

Although the coachhouse has been demolished, the main building has not been substantially altered during the last century. The external walls are of two foot thick random "porphyry," and there is a freestone pilastered entrance porch, flanked by two Doric columns at the front.

The property was acquired by the Church of England in 1899, for Diocesan Offices. It is now preserved as the residences of the Dean and Precentor of Brisbane.

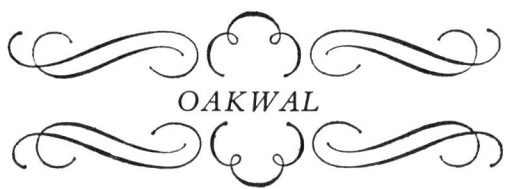

OAKWAL

The hilly suburbs of Brisbane provided many fine sites for the homes of the early dignitaries and well-to-do. Oakwal, built in the early 'sixties at Windsor Heights for Sir James Cockle, Queensland's first Chief Justice, is one of the first and at the same time one of the best preserved of Brisbane's early stone colonial residences. When Sir James and Lady Cockle returned to England, Oakwal was bought by their architect, James Cowlishaw, whose descendants still occupy and have restored it with loving care.

The early Australian buildings, built by English artisans strongly influenced by the Georgian designs current in England at the time of their training, made little allowance for the demands of a very different environment. However, gradually a colonial style evolved which was adapted to the geographical and climatic conditions, and soon it was the accepted practice for the inner rooms of the early homesteads to have access to a wide veranda on three sides and to a detached kitchen wing on the fourth. (This separation of kitchen from living area reduced the fire danger from wood stoves and restricted entry to the private rooms by servants and indentured labour.) The perimeter veranda and spacious, high-ceilinged rooms offered a retreat from the glare and heat outside. Seven foot high cedar louvred shutters shaded and protected the doorways on to the verandas. The early builders made no attempt to raise their houses—this Queensland tradition only developed some forty years later.

Oakwal is built of large squared blocks of Brisbane free-stone with a base of pink "porphyry" rubble. The roof is covered with Welsh slates. Pairs of graceful closely spaced posts support the weight of the slate-roofed veranda and pedimented porch.

19

THE NATIONAL BANK
OF AUSTRALASIA

Gracing the historic corner of Queen Street and Creek Street is a fine piece of classic Italian Renaissance architecture—the Head Office for Queensland of the National Bank of Australasia.

It was on this site that Brisbane's first School of Arts provided a cultural centre for the colony. However, in 1872 financial difficulties forced the school to sell its property for £8,000 to the Queensland National Bank, which united with the National Bank of Australasia in 1948.

Former Colonial Architect, F. D. G. Stanley, was asked to design the new bank—this was his first large private commission. He specified that it should be built in brick with facings and columns of freestone. The foundation stone was laid in 1881 and the bank was ready for occupation four years later. The board room and principal offices are perfectly preserved examples of mid-Victorian opulence. In fact the whole place is an impressive product of a building boom born of unbounded optimism in Queensland's future. It was this same opinion which transformed Brisbane from a frontier town into a colonial city.

Experts hailed it as one of the finest examples of banking architecture anywhere in the world. One contemporary visitor wrote: "No bank in Australia, and the Australian banks were patrons of architecture, had such an imposing façade. The noble colonnade that rose from the spacious balcony on the first floor amazed the few British financiers who visited Brisbane. The banking chamber, domed with stained glass and rich with polished cedar, seemed so magnificent that he wondered whether a customer would dare enter the bank with less than a £10 cheque."

21

BISHOPSBOURNE AND CHAPEL

Bishop Tufnell, Brisbane's first Church of England Bishop, was fortunate in that he did not have to wait long after he arrived to take up his appointment, before some acres of high land at Milton were selected as a suitable site for his official residence and private chapel.

The Lodge, a large square building with Gothic arched verandas, was ready for occupation in 1861. Local "porphyry" stone, relieved by sandstone quoining and arches, was used in its construction.

The original chapel was of timber, but during his episcopate Bishop Donaldson was so determined to have a more permanent building, that he himself paid the considerable difference between the Diocese's contribution and the final cost of a new stone chapel. Dedicated in 1912, the chapel is considered one of the finest works of the architect, Robin Dods, whose designs had a stylistic elegance that greatly influenced Brisbane building in the early part of this century.

Working in the same stone as that already used in the Lodge, he created a ruggedly simple masterpiece in complete harmony with its environment. The chapel is rectangular in plan with a small porch extension at one end. The walls are of 18 inch thick squared blocks, laid at random, with their rough faces left exposed internally and externally. The roof is steeply pitched, covered with slates, and supported by heavy dressed oregon framing stained dark to contrast with the warm colours and natural texture of the walls.

St Francis' Theological College now occupies Bishopsbourne and its outbuildings, which are obscured from view by trees and a large brewery. Recently, the Lodge has been skilfully renovated and converted into administrative offices and flats for the Principal and married staff of the College.

"HIGH STUMP" HOUSES

Queensland's "houses on stilts" attract so much interest that it is worth commenting on their evolution. Many explanations are given for the origins of the style, varying from the very practical to the absurd.

The early house builders of Brisbane kept their floors as close to the ground as possible. It was only in the latter part of the last century, in farming settlements on low coastal land and river flats, that the raised houses first appeared . . . for several excellent reasons. In these localities, the settlers had an abundance of excellent building timbers and found that, by keeping headroom under their houses, they reduced the risk of seasonal flooding and created cheap protection for farm machinery, vehicles, and produce. The greater height from the ground gave their womenfolk a sense of security, which outweighed the burdensome disadvantage of frequent stair climbing during the working day.

Other advantages became evident. The high stumps, with their metal caps, effectively deterred termites, and any such pest infestation could be readily detected and destroyed; they also raised the house above low-flying mosquitoes into breezes unimpeded by undergrowth. Finally, the use of stilts made it possible to build more cheaply on sloping sites. (Unfortunately, on steep slopes the effect of the elongated stumps is sometimes ludicrous.)

The combination of stump base, square plan, perimeter veranda, and pyramidal iron-sheeted roof produced a traditional style. Cast iron balustrades, latticework panels, adjustable wood louvres, and blinds to screen the verandas were later refinements.

25

OLD GOVERNMENT HOUSE

When the time came for building an official residence for the first Governor of Queensland, Sir George Ferguson Bowen, a suitable site was selected in the gardens at the Domain end of George Street.

Tenders, in alternative materials, were invited from three builders and the lowest was accepted. However, the lowest tenderer, realizing that his price was too low, refused to proceed with construction. Joshua Jeays, who was at once architect, builder, and quarry master, was awarded the contract in 1860, for a tender price of £12,000. Sandstone from his Goodna quarry was used for the three main elevations, and Brisbane "porphyry" stone for the rear wall. Later, a further sum of £7,000 was voted for the addition of stables and a guardhouse, which were built under the supervision of Mr John Petrie, a son of the first overseer of works at the Moreton Bay convict settlement.

At that time it was considered Brisbane's stateliest house and it remains a fine piece of architecture. The beautifully proportioned semi-circular portico at the main entrance is particularly distinctive.

Over the years a number of additions were made to the original building, including the roofed piazzas on the north-east and south-west, and the stone *porte-cochère*, built in 1878. In 1895 the whole building complex was renovated.

Between 1862 and 1910 eight successive Governors lived in Old Government House. When the larger official residence was ready for occupation at Rosalie, the building became Queensland's first University.

THE POST OFFICE

The occupants of the first building on Brisbane's General Post Office site were the troublesome ladies of the Female Convict Factory. When they were banished to Eagle Farm in 1837, the Factory was used for a time as a gaol. In 1855 a court building was constructed next to the Factory.

Although Queensland's first Postmaster-General, Mr T. L. Murray-Prior, selected this central Queen Street site for his Post Office in 1862, it was not until 1871 that tenders were invited for the first stage of the building. The contract was awarded to John Petrie, son of Andrew.

With no local architectural heritage, the early English-trained architects simply transplanted the styles and building techniques of their homeland. However, concessions were made to ensure protection from the strong sunlight, and the English tradition was modified by the addition of colonnaded verandas and deeply recessed windows, which produced the typically sub-tropical colonial character seen in many Queensland public buildings.

In 1876 the Police Court, still in use next door, was demolished and the telegraph wing, central archway, and clock tower were added by the original contractor. To maintain the architectural character, the extensions were built of local freestone which matched that of the original building. Although the building has been remodelled internally to conform with the Post Office's changing requirements, the exterior has been carefully preserved. Cleaning and restoration of the stonework has recently been done by the fourth generation of the Petrie firm and at night, skilful floodlighting accentuates every detail of the building's fine design. It will make an impressive background to Brisbane's new central square.

29

BARDON HOUSE

A man of many parts was Joshua Jeays. Not only was he architect, builder, and quarry master, he was also Mayor of Brisbane in 1864, during which time he constructed the foundations of the first bridge over the Brisbane River.

Most of the prominent citizens of early Brisbane, when selecting sites for their homes, were attracted to the many hilltops surrounding the township. Jeays's choice was among the Ashgrove Hills, with fine views to the west and north. He named his property Bardon after Bardon Hill of his native Leicestershire.

The design of his house built in 1853 was just as expressive of nostalgia—there were the same steep gabled roofs with their decorated verges, massive chimneys, and casements, all of which characterized the nineteenth-century English manor houses. It was well built in grey random "porphyry" stone, relieved by arches and quoins of fine tooled and moulded buff freestone. The original split wood shingled roof has been covered by ribbed roofing iron.

Unfortunately, Mrs Jeays died before her house was completed, and her grief-stricken husband, refusing to live there, passed it over to his son.

When the brilliant fourth Premier of Queensland, Sir Charles Lilley, was appointed Chief Justice, he and his wife, who was a daughter of Joshua Jeays, took up residence at Bardon House. Later it was occupied by another Premier, Sir Thomas McIlwraith.

The property is now owned by the Catholic Church and is the home of a teaching order of nuns.

ORMISTON HOUSE

Captain the Honourable Louis Hope, seventh son of the first Earl of Hopetoun, was a man of style. Having purchased an estate of rich coastal land with a view over Raby Bay at Ormiston—he believed that it would become the most beautiful and exclusive suburb of the port—he set about developing it properly so that he could live there in the manner in which he had been accustomed to live. The original house was constructed of planks of pit-sawn cedar, from rain-forests in the district. It still survives as the kitchen wing of the lovely old Ormiston House, built soon after by skilled Scottish artisans, of bricks baked in a kiln on the property.

The board verandas, with roofs supported by pairs of white Doric columns turned out of cedar logs, are only raised one step from the garden. The french lights and their sturdy security shutters, the doors, and the fireplace surrounds are also of red cedar. It is one of the best remaining examples of colonial domestic architecture in the State.

Hope, who also built and supported a small chapel and rectory on his property, became part of our history when, in 1862, he established Australia's first commercial sugar plantation at Ormiston. He brought in South Sea Islanders to cut the cane and built a mill to crush it. This activity did not mean he neglected the garden—in fact he imported £2,000 worth of azaleas from all over the world, and these made the grounds a riot of colour. Parts of the magnificent avenues of palms and pines and an enormous Indian banyan tree, unique in Australia, still survive.

In 1959 the Carmelite nuns acquired the Ormiston estate; it was an ideal place to build their monastery. The old house is to be preserved and will be open for public inspection.

33

WOLSTON HOMESTEAD

Wolston was built between 1852 and 1853 on a rise overlooking the Brisbane River at Wacol. It was the home of the highly cultured and versatile Dr Stephen Simpson, one of the earliest free settlers of Moreton Bay, who filled the posts of Acting Colonial Surgeon, Police Magistrate, member of the Legislative Council, and the first Commissioner of Crown Lands!

In 1860 Wolston was acquired by Mr Matthew Goggs, who later extended it to house his family of twelve, whom he supported by his pastoral and whaling interests. The Grindle family purchased the property from the Goggses in 1907.

The homestead, sheltered by giant fig trees as old, if not older than the building itself, was constructed of local free-stone and hand-made bricks. Red cedar, hand-wrought at the site was used for joinery and framing. (This cedar, plentiful in those days, was often prepared on a site, and it was quite a feature in early country houses.) Full-length verandas protected both the front and rear sides. The large drawing room was divided into two by folding cedar doors. Sandstone steps led down under the main building to the dairy and two cellars, one housing the servants, the other wine casks and stores. These rooms had stone flagged floors and received air and light through small barred openings near their ceilings. The kitchen still retains its baker's oven.

Wolston suffered much damage in the great 1893 flood. It has the distinction of being the first property acquired by the National Trust of Queensland who will make sure the homestead is preserved. The original wood shingle roof has now been replaced by corrugated iron, and other restoration work is proceeding.

OLD COURT HOUSE, CLEVELAND

The abolition of the Moreton Bay penal settlement in 1839, raised the question—hotly debated—of a suitable site for the capital and port of Moreton Bay. The present site and Cleveland were the two most discussed. The Sydney authorities and "wool growers" favoured the latter as the chief port, and recommended Ipswich as the business centre. But, from the beginning, the fates were unkind to Cleveland. When Sir George Gipps decided to inspect the area during a visit to the Brisbane settlement in 1842, the ship arrived at low tide, so the proud Governor and his party were forced to flounder through "a hundred yards of deep nastiness" to reach the shore. After that undignified incident, Gipps's official edict supported Brisbane's claim. Later, Governor Fitz Roy's visit to Cleveland had to be abandoned because of unfavourable weather conditions.

One of the men most disappointed by the edict was Francis Bigge, a squatter, who believed so firmly in the superiority of the Cleveland site that he had built a large brick hotel, still in existence, which became known as Bigge's Folly. He also built a wool store and saw mill, even financed a road direct to Ipswich, and was responsible for getting the jetty and Customs House established there.

The old Court House, built of hand-made brick by Bigge in 1854, and used by him as a place in which to conduct weekly church services, was leased to the Government for a police court and lockup. In 1961 it was carefully restored for use as tea-rooms for tourists.

Once it had been rejected as the capital city, Cleveland faded from public notice. Soon it was known only as a quiet fishing village and, after Sandgate became popular, as a watering place for the fashionable "buggy set."

37

MOONEY MEMORIAL FOUNTAIN

It was most unfortunate that fire broke out in Hughes's Queen Street grocery on that Friday evening in March 1877, because the turncock at the reservoir had just turned off the water supply for the week-end!

However, the volunteer firemen of the City Brigade turned out and salvaged what stores they could until tragedy struck. The heat of the fire exploded a cask of spirits over 22-year-old James Mooney, a native of New York, causing such severe burns that he died.

Public sympathy was immediately aroused, and the citizens of Brisbane were invited to subscribe to a fund to build an appropriate memorial to the brave young fireman. The Brisbane Council opened the appeal, contributing £200 towards the cost of a stone fountain to be set among shade trees at the corner of Queen and Eagle Streets. They also offered a £10 prize for the best fountain design submitted in a public competition, but rejected all the entries. Eventually, however, the City Engineer's design, in the Decorated Gothic style, was approved, and tenders for the building of the monument were invited.

Although Mr W. Webster's tender of £370 exceeded the limit set by the Council, it was accepted and the fountain was unveiled in 1880. Apparently the contractor had much in common with our present generation of bulldozer operators, because, to the dismay of the Council and despite their frequent warnings, he cut down the trees surrounding the memorial. . . . However, they were replaced and now provide a shady retreat for many people working in the tall office blocks near by.

38

39

COLONIAL STORE

Local stone, adzed ironbark girders, pit-sawn yellowwood floorboards, and the sweat of hundreds of toiling convicts went into the old Government Commissariat Store in William Street, opposite Queen's Wharf. The building was begun in 1828—Brisbane at that time was a village of no more than ten cottages—and finished a year later.

Although the roof was subsequently raised for the addition of another storey, the building is practically in its original condition. The workmanship displayed suggests that there were skilled artisans among the convict workmen, because, before Andrew Petrie was appointed colonial overseer of works, only army officers were available to direct the works.

When the convicts were disembarked at Queen's Wharf the store was also used as "a place of detention and correction." Small barred prison windows are still in evidence.

On the cessation of convict transportation, the building served as a migrant depot for ten years. During the "Bread or Blood" riots of 1861, its doors were fitted with iron shutters as a precaution, but fortunately they were not required.

It was a bonded store until Brisbane's first Customs House was built and, as late as 1934, was the storehouse for the prison settlement on St Helena Island in Moreton Bay.

BELLEVUE HOTEL

Stroll down George Street, past the mellowed stone government buildings, and on towards the Botanical Gardens, and you will find the Bellevue Hotel faced on opposite corners by its distinguished neighbours, Parliament House and the Queensland Club. Set among huge fig trees and jacarandas, these buildings have created a serene environment normally associated with a more gracious age.

After the opening of the new Parliament House on the opposite corner, the first section of the Bellevue was built; it offered "private apartments for families and gentlemen and good stable accommodation."

Of great interest to overseas visitors and pastoralists because of its uniquely Australian atmosphere, the Bellevue owes its unspoilt charm to the determination of a succession of owners. Each one was prepared to go to great lengths to prevent the original architectural character being destroyed, and although there have been several internal remodellings and renovations over the years, the external appearance has been maintained.

Much of the Bellevue's character is derived from the delicate tracery of the cast iron balustrades, valances, and columns screening the deep verandas on each floor. This was characteristic of many Australian buildings of this period. Not only was an air of opulence in tune with the times, cheaply imparted by these mass-produced cast iron panels, but they provided some protection from strong sunlight, without impeding cooling breezes. The Sydney *Bulletin* aptly described the Bellevue as "a glorious colonial pub with its starched lace skirts properly picked out in white, its corrugated roofs curving down as plumply as a 'nineties belle.'"

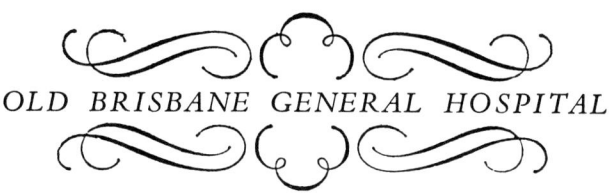

OLD BRISBANE GENERAL HOSPITAL

In the early days of settlement Brisbane people were struck down by all kinds of diseases, many of which have since been virtually eliminated. "Colonial fevers" and tuberculosis took a heavy toll, particularly among migrants and the South Sea Islanders brought to Queensland to work in the sugar cane fields. And, judging by the number of patients treated for gunshot and stabbing wounds, early Brisbane must have had its fair share of Wild Colonial Boys!

In any case, the demands for hospital facilities were too great for the colony's first public hospital, which had been established in George Street in 1849, so a site for a larger one was selected in The Quarries at Herston. These quarries, which were once worked by convict gangs, provided much of the stone used in the early Brisbane buildings.

It was intended that the first section of the new hospital, built in 1867 to accommodate 109 patients, should be supported on one hand by voluntary contributions and on the other by whatever sum the patients could afford, but financial difficulties soon made it necessary for the Queensland Government to assume control. This first section still forms part of a teaching, research, and training hospital complex that has grown to one of the largest in the Southern Hemisphere.

The original building was designed by the Colonial Architect, Charles Tiffin, who pleaded with the authorities to abandon the "Old Country" style of hospital and allow him to design a building more suited to the Brisbane climate, with maximum ventilation and generous verandas. Fortunately, his plea was listened to and the brick and stone hospital illustrated resulted.

THE JOSS HOUSE, BREAKFAST CREEK

A part of Brisbane with a colourful history is Breakfast Creek, named by Lieutenant John Oxley, who breakfasted there in 1823 on his cruise of discovery up the Brisbane River. On the south bank of the creek, Newstead House became the gay centre for Brisbane's pioneer society, but the opposite side has a startling record of violence.

Incongruously set between a racecourse and a community of people of Italian descent, many of them still fishermen and bait merchants, is Brisbane's only Chinese Buddhist Temple.

Built in 1884 by local Chinese market-gardeners and supported by a few of their countrymen from the Palmer River goldfields, who imported workmen and materials from their homeland, the Joss House was used as a regular meeting place for worship. During the Chinese New Year celebrations, fire crackers were exploded and the local children gathered around for free rice and ginger.

In 1930 it was closed because the younger generation had grown up Christians, and the congregations had dwindled. With the passing of the older Chinese, its ownership became obscure, and the Joss House degenerated into a doss house for vagrants. Finally it fell into disrepair and was much damaged by vandals, who destroyed its altars, statues, gongs, and bells.

In 1966 Brisbane's Chinese community, concerned about the desecration of their Joss House, formed a Chinese Temple Society to restore and preserve it, both as a historical building and as a place of worship. Special roof tiles, furnishings, and ornaments were imported from Hong Kong and at the most propitious time, 2 a.m. on 13 June 1966, the Triad Holy Temple for Chinese Buddhists was reopened.

47

QUEENSLAND CLUB

Almost to the time of separation from New South Wales, there was much controversy and rivalry over the site for the capital city.

The "squatters" favoured Ipswich as the commercial centre, with Cleveland as its port—the popular centre for this influential element was the North Australian Club of Ipswich. To quote the early diarist, Nehemiah Bartley, who was to become a foundation member of the Queensland Club, the great success of the Ipswich Club "stirred up the Brisbane folks, at the end of 1859, to have a club of their own."

Four days before separation was proclaimed, twenty prominent citizens met and formed a club to be named after the new colony. The Governor was to be patron. The club occupied premises in Mary Street, which accommodated them until 1880 when the land at the corner of George Street and Alice Street was acquired, and an architect member, F. D. G. Stanley, was commissioned to design the new building. The adjoining property in Alice Street was bought in 1889 and made into a bowling green, later to be converted to the tennis court, which is still in use.

Although he had an English classical training, Stanley understood the influences of the Brisbane climate. His design, modelled on that of London's West End clubs, incorporated wide verandas, with french lights leading into the spacious, high-ceilinged rooms, which have all the dignity of more gracious days. In fact, considering the club at that time boasted no more than 202 members the whole building was remarkably imposing. Its grandeur was another indication of the faith people placed in the future of the new State.

49

PARLIAMENT HOUSE

The first Parliament of the Crown Colony of Queensland—this colony was formed when the Moreton Bay District was separated from New South Wales—sat for more than eight years in the convict barracks in Queen Street.

It was obviously necessary to have a proper Parliament House, so a commission was appointed to select an architect, and in 1864 they decided to hold an Australia-wide design competition. The generous premium of 200 guineas was won by Mr Charles Tiffin, Queensland's Colonial Architect. He designed this gracious building in a modified French Renaissance style, of a less ornate character than was usual at that period. The arched colonnades were not part of his initial design; they were added in 1880.

The foundation stone for the original building was laid in 1865 (it was not until August three years later that the first Parliament was summoned to meet in the completed Parliament House). The contractor was Mr Joshua Jeays, who cut the freestone for the external walls in his own quarry near Ipswich. In the spacious interior generous use was made of the finest Canungra cedar, polished and rubbed to a satin finish. The main circular staircase was erected by a method that had never been used before.

The George Street façade is 304 feet long and rises to a height of 103 feet. The Alice Street wing was added in 1891. The total cost of both wings rose to £100,000, which, at about £1,000 a room, was a huge expenditure at that time.

Palms and jacarandas in the forecourt cast a lacework of shadows on the walls, which have become more beautiful with the mellowing of age.

51

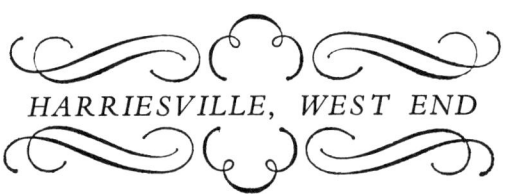

HARRIESVILLE, WEST END

Serenely set among magnificent pine trees on the riverside at West End is Harriesville, generally considered to be Brisbane's best surviving example of early colonial domestic timber architecture. Unlike many of its contemporaries, which have been demolished or unsympathetically remodelled, Harriesville is lovingly preserved by its present owner; it is surrounded by well-tended gardens and lawns sweeping down to the water's edge.

Built in 1872 by Mr Eustace Harries, chief draughtsman of the Colonial Architect's Office, this house demonstrates how the early designers and craftsmen, steeped in the traditional proportions and symmetry of the Georgian period, successfully adapted this style to the climatic conditions of the colonies.

After the death of Mr Harries, the house had several distinguished tenants, but the original family resumed residence in 1888. During the great 1893 flood the furniture and outbuildings were swept away, but although the swirling water rose to the level of the fanlights, the house was saved because someone had the foresight to leave the french lights leading to the verandas open.

The steep pyramidal roof, built entirely of timber, was originally covered with wood shingles, but they were later replaced by the ubiquitous corrugated iron. The graceful pairs of posts supporting the curved iron of the veranda roof contrast with the wide, hand-wrought chamfer boards lining the walls. The internal fittings and joinery, even part of the framing, are of red cedar, which was then plentiful in the forests south of Brisbane.

UNITED SERVICE INSTITUTE, VICTORIA BARRACKS

Tucked away in a corner of the Victoria Barracks, there is as quaint a relic of Victoriana as you would come across on any day's march. Originally built as stables for the mounted police, it became the quarters for horse-drawn ambulances when military barracks were established in Petrie Terrace. Later it served as stables for a unit of mounted artillery. Beside the entrance there is a polished brass cannon and a sign bearing the date 1865.

This is another building demonstrating that the designers of that period had more than a working knowledge of classic proportions, but shortages of funds and skilled tradesmen forced them to modify details.

The results may not have been scholarly, but the stables—utilitarian as they are—have a simple dignity.

Without any interference to its external character, the building has been converted to accommodate the United Service Institute. The central grooming and saddling area has been covered with a dance floor. Offices, library, and bar occupy the old tack rooms surrounding it.

The original open trussed lantern roof remains unchanged. Over the years a variety of odours have drifted up to it—the smell of stabled horses, leather, and disinfectant have now been replaced by the perfumes of the officers' ladies on party nights.

SOUTH BRISBANE TOWN HALL

The Municipality of Brisbane, created in 1859, included within its boundaries South Brisbane. However, the fact that this area was separated from the City of Brisbane by the river caused so much rivalry and division of interests that in 1888 the "Southsiders" petitioned to have the adjacent wards of South Brisbane and Woolloongabba amalgamated to form the Borough of South Brisbane. The petition was successful, and the "Southside" developed rapidly, especially after the establishment of industries and the extension of deep-water wharf facilities.

In the early days, the borough administration was housed in a modest brick building, now part of a flour mill, but this soon proved inadequate. So in 1892, the ambitious Town Hall, designed by John Hall and Sons and costing £11,000, was constructed on a slope overlooking the river. Built of red brick relieved by freestone features it expressed a maturity of civic pride long before the Greater Brisbane City Council was contemplated.

At that period, it was considered a social necessity for Town Halls to have ornate clock towers, but there is nothing ponderous or baroque about the design of this one. Although it is in a romantic style, there is much sophistication in the handling of the fenestration and of the details generally.

When the Greater Brisbane City Council, with centralized administration, was created in 1924, the suburban town halls became superfluous. The South Brisbane Town Hall served many purposes. First it was a Works Depot; then it was converted into flats for the families of Council engineers recruited from England, and it is now—more fittingly, since it is such a dignified building—the home of the Queensland Conservatorium of Music.

56

STORY BRIDGE

In 1839 when the last of the inmates of "His Majesty's Department of Correction" were removed from the Moreton Bay District, Governor Gipps dispatched his surveyors "to lay out a township and parcel out country land for occupation."

An area of flat land, bounded on three sides by a loop in the Brisbane River, was selected as the site for the "township." The principal surveyor, who had lived in Batavia, planned to emulate that city's wide streets, open spaces, and generous public squares.

Unfortunately, after an inspection of the town site, Governor Gipps vetoed the surveys and left Brisbane with a heritage of narrow, congested streets, laid out in a conventional gridiron plan bearing little relationship to the winding river, destined to become Australia's greatest commercial watercourse.

This lack of initial planning has resulted in a dearth of bridges. The first major bridge was the Story which linked the Valley end of the city with Kangaroo Point. Second in size only to the Sydney Harbour Bridge, it was commenced in 1935 and opened in 1939. Its location greatly pleased the Valley traders who realized that much of the "Southside" traffic would be diverted past their stores. It was constructed to the design of Dr J. C. Bradfield by two Brisbane firms, Evans Deakin and Hornibrook Constructions, and financed by an insurance company. The massive abutments were built with river gravel and cement made from coral dredged near the river's mouth.

Millions are now being spent on resumptions to create open spaces in the city, and on the building of new bridges and distributor roads to relieve cross-city traffic.

CUSTOMS HOUSE

Soon after the Moreton Bay District was officially opened to free settlement in 1842, the development of wharf facilities for maritime trade commenced. In 1846 Brisbane was declared a port of entry and clearance, and a branch of the Customs Department was established.

While the controversy raged over the relative merits of Cleveland and Brisbane as sites for the State's capital, the Customs House operated from the Commissariat Store.

In 1848 the present site in Petrie Bight was selected by Captain Owen Stanley, not without many protests from the ships' captains, who complained that to report and clear their vessels, they had to walk a mile through the bush from their South Brisbane berths.

By 1884 the original Customs House and rented bond premises had become quite inadequate for the rapidly growing port, and the Colonial Architect was instructed to design a new building "which would have a beautiful appearance from both Queen Street and the River."

Mr Charles McLay ably designed the building and supervised construction by John Petrie and Son. It is still regarded as one of the most handsome and best situated Customs Houses in the world. It is built of local freestone, and is 150 feet long and 75 feet wide; the design features a colonnaded entrance between twin pedimented wings on front and rear façades, surmounted by a copper sheathed dome. No expense was spared in the fitting out of the elegant cruciform-shaped Long Room and the interior appointments generally.

The massive staircase and joinery were of polished red cedar, contrasting with imported Italian marbles and English ornamental ironwork.

THE TREASURY

Before the establishment of the Moreton Bay settlement in 1824, there was not one white settler in the vast expanse which is now Queensland.

In 1839 the penal settlement at Moreton Bay was closed down, to the relief of all concerned, and the district was thrown open to free men.

When moves for separation from New South Wales were started in 1852, the *Sydney Herald* scornfully wrote: "It is difficult to mete out the portions of laughter, pity, and contempt which must be awarded to our misguided fellow-colonists lying to the northward of the thirtieth degree of latitude. . . ."

Only a relatively short time elapsed between first settlement and the creation of the self-governing state of Queensland in 1859, and this is remarkable, particularly in view of the unpropitious financial start—Queensland's first Governor, Sir George Ferguson Bowen, found 7½d. in the Treasury when he took office in 1859. Even that was stolen two days later! However, in 1888, no less than £94,647 was voted for building the first stage of the Treasury Building at North Quay, on the site of the original military barracks.

This imposing Renaissance building was designed by the Government Architect at that time, J. J. Clark. He selected a light grey sandstone for the exterior walls to ensure the maximum play of light and shade on his delicate details.

Brisbane is fortunate that the restored Treasury Building is being preserved, because it is an important element in the imposing line of government buildings of local stone extending down George Street, which makes such a contribution to the character of the city.

SOMERVILLE HOUSE

When T. B. Stephens, a Lancashire wool expert, went to Brisbane for a short visit in 1860, he found a township of bullock-tracks and mud. . . . But he was shrewd enough to see that there was money to be made by the enterprising. He stayed to become one of the colony's first mayors. During his twenty years in Parliament, he was also Colonial Secretary, Postmaster-General, and Secretary for Lands, and, as if that wasn't enough, he owned two newspapers.

At that time, at the close of each day, a curfew bell warned the Aborigines to return to their camps located beyond the "Blacks' Poles" erected at a prudent distance on the north and south of the township. The one for the south side was on a hill overlooking South Brisbane and Woolloongabba. It was on this high ground that T. B. Stephens bought 16 acres—the site for the home which he built in 1870 for his Lancashire bride. He named the property Cumbooquepa, the Aboriginal name for the adjacent waterholes.

However, when the South Coast railway line was built, the house and half the land were resumed. Stephen's eldest son William built a new Cumbooquepa on the remaining land. It was then Brisbane's largest private residence, a grandiose E-shaped red brick mansion with steep slated roofs, marble floors, vaulted ceilings, and stained glass windows depicting Shakespearian characters.

The Stephens family lived there until 1905, after which it was a boarding house until 1919, when the Presbyterian and Methodist Churches bought it to convert it into a high school for girls. The lagoons were filled to form playing fields.

In honour of a nineteenth-century Scottish woman educator, the property was named Somerville House and is now one of Brisbane's largest independent girls' schools.

GOVERNMENT HOUSE

Johann Christian Heussler, a native of Frankfurt, was thirty-four when he arrived in Brisbane in 1854. In addition to being a merchant and pioneer sugar planter, he was a very public-spirited man, and became a Justice of the Peace, Consul for Germany and the Netherlands, and a member of the Legislative Council.

He also secured his place in Queensland's history by returning to his homeland to organize the migration of hard-working German farmers, who so successfully developed the districts in which they settled, and by building a home which he named Fernberg and which was destined to form the original portion of the present Government House. The site he chose for Fernberg was a wooded hilltop at Rosalie, accessible only by a steep track from Milton. However, the Heussler family had only been in their grand two-storey residence for seven years when reverses in the sugar industry forced them to sell Fernberg. This was in 1872.

It had three more occupants before a wealthy grazier, John Stevenson, M.L.A., bought it for his town house. He enlarged the grounds and added a new wing which incorporated the tower flanked by the distinctive bays of bow windows.

When the old Government House on the Domain became too small for its purpose in 1910, the State acquired Fernberg, and Sir William McGregor became the first Governor to live there. Extensions to two wings were made in 1937. The building, set in 44 acres of gardens and thickly wooded grounds, has recently been renovated and a swimming pool has been added. It now has six bedrooms, two sitting rooms, a reception room, a dining room, and a library.

GOLD COAST AND
GREEN MOUNTAINS

Drawings by
KEVIN JOPSON

Text by
PETER NEWELL

CONTENTS

70

THE SEEKERS

Whoever strolls among the pleasure-seekers on the Gold Coast must strain his imagination to the utmost to see it as it was before they came. Few places in Australia have had the past so rapidly overlaid by the present, and yet the story of the area is as colourful as the crowds who flaunt their holiday garb along the beaches. Long before it became the nation's most popular tourist resort, with a perpetual carnival atmosphere offering everything from boomerang-throwing lessons to a speedcar circuit, it was regarded as rich land for development. The climate has a tropical equanimity which is only rarely shattered by cyclones, and to the early settlers the whole district offered wealth to those who would work for it.

The coastline which stretches from Coolangatta in the south to Southport in the north was first described by Lieutenant James Cook. Sailing northwards in May 1770, he brought the *Endeavour* within three miles of the surf. For him and his crew, the creaming white lines held no promise of pleasure. They were breakers on a dangerous shoal, and for the benefit of future navigators he marked their position by naming and charting Point Danger and Mount Warning, describing the latter as "sufficiently conspicuous to be at

once distinguished from every other object" amongst the "high and hilly land" on which it stood.

These coastal ranges from which Mount Warning protrudes, and which cup the Gold Coast between their green slopes and the sea, were given a name by the explorer Allan Cunningham. During his 1827 expedition he blazed the trail across the Darling Downs and through the Great Dividing Range, and saw the mountains from inland. He called them the McPherson Ranges, as a compliment to Major Duncan McPherson.

The *Endeavour* may have been watched by people of the Ugarapul, Wangerriburra, and Kombumerri tribes, who lived along the coastline which Lieutenant Cook observed. They were a sleek, well-fed race, mentally and physically superior to the inland tribes who had to wander in a ceaseless search for food. Living in fertile country, well-stocked with bush tucker and with rivers teeming with fish and eels, they lived peacefully within their tribal boundaries. For a change of diet, there were oysters and eugaries along the shore, and where they feasted the middens have been found under the sand.

Perhaps they regarded the white sails beyond the white surf as some kind of an omen, although it was not until 1824 that the first white community settled in Queensland.

These were the men whom their commander, Captain Patrick Logan, described scornfully as "deep-dyed and twice-convicted felons," when he was given charge of the penal settlement at Moreton Bay. It had been established on the recommendation of John Oxley, who discovered the Tweed River in 1823. Its mouth had been obscured from Cook by the shoals and breakers.

Captain Logan explored his domain as vigorously as he disciplined the convicts. His first discoveries were the Logan River and the mouth of the Nerang River, which is now known as the Broadwater at Southport. He also fixed the correct position of the peak which Cook had called Mount Warning.

He wrote enthusiastically about the plains through which the Logan and Albert Rivers flowed to the sea, saying that

"... the country ... exceeded my most sanguine expectations and is everywhere exceedingly well-watered and, I have no doubt, whenever it may suit the views of the Government to open it for settlers, it will be found the most desirable district for that purpose hitherto found in the colony."

The views of the Government did not turn in this direction until 1842. Until then, the whole area for fifty miles around Brisbane was closed to free settlement, even though convict transportation ceased in 1839.

Captain Logan was mysteriously murdered on his last expedition, just before his regiment was to be relieved, but his report on what was then known as the Northern Districts of the Crown Colony of New South Wales lived after him. It inspired three men, the Lawless brothers and William

Pioneer's Chapel — Mudgeeraba

Cedar Hauliers Cottage — Numinbah

Humphreys, to make an epic journey from Sydney as soon as the area was opened for settlement.

Driving a great mob of sheep and horses, they followed the route explored by Allan Cunningham and Patrick Leslie— who had become the first settler on the Darling Downs. Riding up through Cunningham's Gap, they looked out over the enormous green panorama which slopes away towards the sea. This was the Promised Land indeed, and no one can ever know again the kind of thrilling excitement with which men must have surveyed it. Its lush fertility promised wealth which would be far more solidly based than any gold rush.

Descending from the ranges, they travelled about fifty miles to the east, and selected two adjoining pastoral properties along the west bank of the Albert River. This was the district to become the thriving country centre known as Beaudesert; a "beautiful wilderness."

74

The three settlers were soon followed by others. In the same year, depasturing licences were issued to several more squatters, and the development of Queensland's most historic grazing district had begun.

Rich though the land might be, it was desperately short of one essential: men. Deprived of ticket-of-leave men and time-expired convicts, the squatters sought vainly for labour to work on their properties. A group of them even sought to restore the importation of convicts, under the euphemism of "exiles," but were defeated by the opposition of Church, press, and merchants.

The "floating pest houses" of immigrant ships discharged their human cargoes in Sydney, where most of them found work. Even the migrants destined for the Northern Districts did not always get there, and when the gold rushes began it was even harder to tempt them northwards.

To some extent, the situation was relieved by the Irish famine of 1846, which caused massive emigration to this and other parts of the New World, but it was a solution which did not please everyone. Dr Dunmore Lang, who had founded the first Lutheran Missionary settlement near Brisbane, and who was known as "the clerical agitator with the acid tongue," became concerned about the country becoming "a mere province of Popedom." In 1849 he organized the Cooksland Colonization Company, to bring in shiploads of worthy Presbyterian migrants. Taking with him samples of Brisbane-grown cotton, he returned to England on a recruiting campaign. The samples of cotton impressed Manchester merchants, and his glowing descriptions of the colony attracted a nucleus of sturdy migrants.

Other colonization schemes were less reputable. Chinese migrants were indentured for £10 per annum as shepherds, but as soon as the selections were fenced they became market gardeners. Captain Robert Towns, a Sydney merchant and pastoralist, bought his labour even more cheaply. He recruited Pacific Islanders, known as Kanakas, to work his cotton plantation on the Logan. The press accused him of introducing the slave trade into Australia, but his example was followed by others. Recruited by "blackbirders," often under conditions of savage trickery and cruelty, the Kanakas were imported for 10/- a month and rations, and soon became a familiar sight on the farms.

After years of protesting by missionaries and journalists, the blackbirding trade was stopped by the government. Most of the Kanakas returned to their islands, but a few families remained in the Tweed district.

A group of German migrants was brought out by Johann Christian Heussler, of Frankfurt. He arrived first, in 1854, and was so impressed by the country that he returned home to enlist farmers to work the sugar plantations. They proved to be frugal and industrious, and it was said of them that, although the kangaroos ate out the English settlers, the Germans ate out the kangaroos. The Beenleigh district, originally known as German Pocket, is still populated by descendants of Heussler's migrant families.

The labour problem was solved when, after 1860, the migrant ships sailed straight into Moreton Bay, and the gold rushes petered out. By that time, settlement had spread a good deal further, and white men had penetrated into the forested ranges which, until then, had only known the soft step of the Aborigines.

Among the first exploiters of the Gold Coast's natural wealth were the cedar-getters. As early as the 1830s, these hard-drinking, hard-working men had pushed up the coast as far as the Tweed River. The handsome red cedar wood had first been felled along the Hunter River, and had become much in demand by cabinet-makers. The cedar-getters worked out the stands along the Hunter, Clarence, Richmond, and Tweed Rivers, and pushed back into the unknown mountains and the headwaters of the rivers.

Two of them, William Duncan and Edmund Harper, moved from the Tweed to the Nerang River as soon as the district was open for settlement. They ranged into the mountains in search of cedars and beeches, which were felled, sawn into manageable lengths, and taken to the streams. The logs were floated down to the rafting grounds at Harper's Wharf, on the Tallebudgera, and the mouth of the Nerang. Large rafts of cedar logs were even taken through

the bar of the Tweed, and then drifted up on the northerly
ocean current to the Nerang bar. Here they were linked to
rafts assembled on the Broadwater, until some of them were
as much as half-a-mile long. Steam tugs towed them to the
Brisbane River for milling or export.

Most of the beautiful trees have now gone for ever. The
timber-cutters were merciless in their assault on the forests
which had taken centuries to reach maturity. They even
cut down trees in places inaccessible to the bullock-teams,
which could not drag them to the streams. Decaying cedar
logs are still found in remote gorges, and a few have been
recovered.

The record cedar was cut in 1898, and hauled into Nerang
by the bullockies Guinea and Burns. Before being squared, its
butt measured thirty-four feet in diameter, and one of its
logs was exhibited in Paris and London.

While the cedar-getters were destroying the natural
vegetation, other men were introducing plants which would

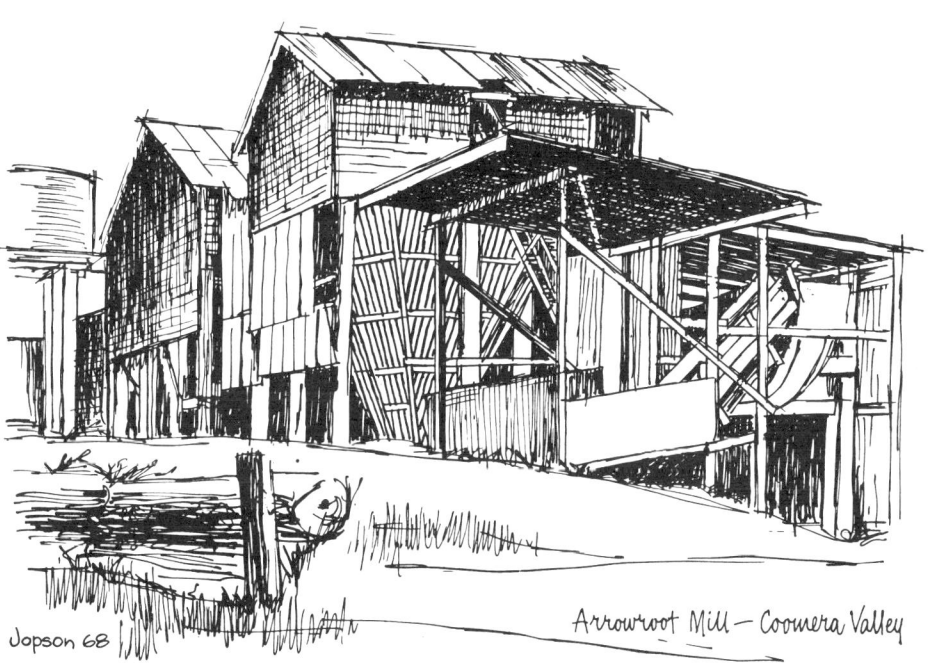

Jopson 68

Arrowroot Mill – Coomera Valley

flourish in its deep soil and opulent sunshine. These were cotton, sugar, arrowroot, and bananas.

Experimental plots of cotton, from the Sea Islands off Georgia in the U.S.A, had been grown around Brisbane since the earliest days of settlement. When the energetic Dr Dunmore Lang returned to England to crusade for his "Colony of Cooksland," he took samples of the cotton to demonstrate the potential of the country. As soon as his colonists arrived, he assisted them to take up land along the Logan and Albert Rivers, and advised them to clear the rich scrublands and plant cotton. This, he said, would "combine righteousness with sound business," by helping to strike a blow at slavery in the U.S.A. The first shipment of cotton was exported in 1854, and the infant industry boomed when the Civil War cut off American supplies to the Manchester cotton mills.

Captain Towns, the importer of Kanakas, established a

Jopson 68.

cotton plantation on 4,000 acres along the Logan River. This was in 1863, and he employed 260 Kanakas as field-hands. Other cotton companies were established at Pimpama and Nerang, the latter in the area now occupied by dairy farms, water-ski gardens, and a car-racing circuit.

King Cotton's rule was brief. When the Civil War ended, shipments recommenced across the shorter ocean haul from the southern states of America to England, and the Gold Coast farmers turned to sugar, arrowroot, and dairy farming.

John Buhot was the first man to extract sugar from cane grown in the colony, but Captain the Hon. Louis Hope, on his bayside property at Ormiston, was the first to grow and crush sugar in commercial quantities. He pioneered the new industry in 1862, and received government encouragement in the form of 2,560 acres on the Coomera River, now Hope Island, on which to establish new plantations.

Sugar Mill—Woongoolba

In those days, cotton and sugar were "slave crops," and planters had grown rich on the work of Negroes imported into America and the West Indies. There was no such supply of cheap labour available in Australia, so Captain Hope also recruited Kanakas to work on his plantations. Cane grown in the district was found to have the world's highest sugar content, though the juice had to be extracted in primitive mills built by the canegrowers. But in 1864 a visitor compared an early mill with the long-established ones of Natal and Mauritius, and wrote ". . . upon close inspection. I found it to possess every requisite necessary for the manufacture of sugar. The mill has been fitted up with the greatest regard to economy of both space and material, which indicates the presence not only of a careful, but a master hand."

One of those who worked on building the early mills was Francis Lahey, who set up a sawbench to cut bush timber for the boiling vats around Pimpama. From his one-man industry has grown the huge timber firm developed by his sons.

Sugar-growing flourished until the 1870s, when sugar prices dropped and a succession of severe winters damaged the cane. Many sugar mills between the Logan and Tweed Rivers were forced to close down, and today only one remains. This is at Woongoolba, where it also produces molasses from local cane for the Beenleigh rum distillery. The Beenleigh district is estimated to have an annual potential of 200,000 tons of cane.

Settlers with small holdings and even smaller capital, who had to rely on their own and their families' labour, found that they could make a good living by cultivating the lily-like plants of the arrowroot. Introduced from the West Indies, it produced enormous yields to the acre when planted in the loamy soil of the river flats. The bulbs contain an easily-digestible starch, which in the nineteenth century was greatly esteemed as an invalid food and is nowadays used in commercial food preparation and in the making of industrial adhesives. The settlers devised ingenious plants for extracting the starch from the bulbs, and the earliest mill for processing arrowroot in commercial quantities was built at Pimpama

Pioneer Cottage — Advancetown

81

Farmhouse — Beenleigh

by the Lahey family. Their patented method of mechanical milling is still used today, in the two mills which wash, grate, and sun-dry the total Australian supply of arrowroot.

Maize, which thrived in the moist, warm climate, was another cash crop for the smaller farmer. The demand for maize products, for stock food, starch, and "Johnny Cake," grew so rapidly that in 1888 the district produced two million bushels.

Bananas, also from the West Indies, have been grown on Gold Coast hillsides for many years, but whatever type of crop they chose to raise, the life of the early settlers was hard. Clearing the dense scrub, which grew in a jungle profusion on hillsides soaked by centuries of sun and rain, was a back-breaking start to a new life in a new country, and they had no time or money for refinements.

The homes of the early days were built from the materials and with the tools at hand. For the cedar-getters and the first selectors, the handiest tool was an axe, and they lived in bark humpies. When drays and trading vessels brought them adzes, hammers, cross-cut saws, wedges and mauls, they were able to plan more ambitious dwellings. Walls and floors were wide slabs, split from straight-grained ironbarks. The wall slabs were fitted horizontally into a framework of bush timber, in much the same method used by modern frame-and-panel prefabrication systems. The roofs were either made from bark, secured by saplings, or of split hardwood shingles.

Life inside such houses was as rough-and-ready as their outside appearance. There might be two rooms, of which one was for sleeping and the other for cooking, eating, and general living. Beds were made of sacks, slung upon sapling frames, and the rest of the furniture was made of packing cases or knocked together from slabs and posts. The settlers had to wage a constant battle against mosquitoes, ants, snakes, and the myriad of flying insects which came in through the unglazed, unscreened windows and the chinks in the walls. The women cooked over an open fire, which was never allowed to go out, in a cooking recess which, with its chimney, was for safety's sake detached from the house. Cauldrons were suspended from a hook over an antbed fireplace. Later, a separate kitchen was built at the rear. The only concession to "gracious living" was a front veranda, to give the house a little shade and to protect the saddle racks.

For the settler who did not even know how to start building his house, do-it-yourself instructions were available. *Mrs. Ransom's Australian Enquiry Book* contained plans, specifications, and a list of materials for a four-room slab house. The estimated cost was £30—which included the purchase of tools. The women were urged to assist their husbands by lining the interiors with burlap, making "wall pockets for newspapers, polished horns and skeleton leaves," and decorating the walls with pages from illustrated magazines.

A typical example of a pioneer's slab hut can be seen at Advancetown, and another has been re-erected by the Historical Society at Beaudesert. But as time went by, and the farms and grazing properties began to show a profit, the slab huts were replaced by the typical Queensland country houses. Square in plan, they were framed and clad in sawn hardwood, with internal partitions of one-inch pine boards. There was plenty of excellent building timber in the bush, but the pyramidal roofs, originally covered with timber shingles, were later covered with corrugated iron to reduce fire danger and insurance premiums. The box-like appearance of the houses was softened by verandas on all sides, on which the inhabitants enjoyed outdoor living long before the phrase was invented by real estate salesmen.

Even more characteristic of Queensland are the high-stump houses, which were at first built for the very practical reason of keeping the floor level above flood level. They were at first built in districts where flooding was a fairly regular occurrence, and the sheltered space beneath them became a handy storage area for fodder, tools, and vehicles. The kitchen was sometimes in a separate wing, connected to the house by a covered walkway.

When the larger landowners decided that the time was ripe to exchange their slab huts for something more befitting their station, they favoured more imposing and individual designs than the four-square country houses. Nowadays these are known as "Squatters' houses;" an odd term, derived from the semi-contemptuous description of a man who seized a piece of land which suited him by settling upon it and claiming squatter's rights. But contempt turned to respect when the squatters were men like William Humphreys and the Lawless brothers; Clement and Paul. Vigorous, adventurous, and courageous, they overlanded their flocks for

Jopson

hundreds of miles through almost untrodden territory to pioneer the "Northern Districts." It was almost as though they were obeying some deep instinct which gave them unbounded faith in the future. They must have known that it would be many years before the population of Queensland— or even of Australia—could support a large grazing industry. Nearly half-a-century was to pass before refrigerated meat could be shipped overseas, wool prices were often so low that it was hardly worth shearing the sheep, and much of their stock finished in the tallow pots. A series of droughts in the 1860s culminated in a serious financial depression, and the Lands Act of 1868 halved the selectors' holdings. But with the same dogged persistence which had brought their flocks through the plains and mountains, they held on to what they had carved out of the wilderness.

Pioneer Farm Buildings — Nerang Valley

Early Holiday House — Southport Esplanade

William Humphreys gave his selection the name of Mundoolun, and built himself a three-roomed cottage of split hardwood slabs roofed with grass thatch. His glowing prophecies of the district's future attracted his relations, John and Anne Collins, from Sydney, and in 1844 they arrived by bullock-dray with their two young children. Another slab cottage was built for them, and they lived in it until 1847, when Humphreys decided to take up land further north. John Collins took over Mundoolun, and employed a ship's carpenter to rebuild and extend the original cottage, to accommodate his growing family.

The hardwood slabs were replaced by fourteen inch by two inch planks, pitsawn from the fine cedars which still stood along the banks of the river. Although the house has been improved and restored several times the original slab walls, and the sawpit, still remain. Mundoolun became the social centre for the pioneers of the district, and has been occupied and cherished ever since. The present owners are Mr and Mrs Douglas Fraser, who built a new residence overlooking the lagoon and moved into it before the second world war. The original homestead is now the home of their son, Mr William Fraser, and his family is the fifth generation to have lived in it during more than a century.

On a rise overlooking Mundoolun Station, near Tamborine Village, the descendants of John and Anne Collins built a church in their memory. Consecrated in 1901 as the Church of St John the Evangelist, it contains a memorial tablet in the sanctuary which explains why such a substantial stone church should be found in a place which apparently has no parish to support it. It is a fitting tribute to the faith and fortitude of John Collins and his wife Anne, who emigrated from Ireland to seek their fortune in Australia and lived at Mundoolun for fifty years. Although William Humphreys took up the selection, the Collins family transformed the virgin forest, which had been the hunting ground

"Mundoolun" Homestead — Tamborine Valley

of the Wangerriburra tribe, into the splendid grazing property which is still being worked by their descendants. Beside the family graves in the churchyard is that of Bullumm, the last of the Wangerriburras.

St John's was designed by John H. Buckeridge, who at that time was the diocesan architect of Brisbane. Of a simple Gothic style, with a square tower, it was built of light brown sandstone quarried on the property, with furnishings and ceiling of local red cedar.

St. John's of "Mundoolun"

William Humphrey's companions, Clement and Paul Lawless, settled in a beautiful valley at the head of the Albert River, overlooked by two spurs of the McPherson Ranges. But they lived there for only four years, and in 1846 they transferred the lease of the property, which they had named Nindooinbah, to Arthur William Compigne, who later sold it to the versatile Captain Robert Towns. The Lawless brothers moved on to settle in the Burnett district.

Nindooinbah was sold twice more before it became the home of William Collins, the first white child born on the Albert. The first homestead was built about 1865, and in 1908 the eminent Brisbane architect, Robin Dods, was engaged to add nursery and guest wings and to replace the detached kitchen with a service wing. He maintained the character of the original building, and matched its wide, hand-wrought cedar chamferboards and distinctive balustrading. The deep verandas are supported by stout hardwood posts, painted white to contrast with the brown timbers. The original drawing-room still contains the cedar furniture and appointments which were the pride of the family in late Victorian days, and the furniture of the guest wing was made from a bunya pine which was removed to make way for the extension.

The charming panelled dining room has a vaulted ceiling decorated by the wife of the architect, who also incised the sandstone arch of the fireplace with the beautifully carved words: *The garden is gay in the month of May, the fire is the flower of the winter's day.*

The stately old homestead, surrounded by acres of lawns and gardens, is now the home of Mrs de Burgh Persse, a descendant of William Collins, and her daughter Margaret.

The homestead of Coochin-Coochin has an unusual history. The original house was built in the early 1840s, about eight miles away from its present location, with walls and ceilings of local pitsawn cedar and floors of hand-wrought hardwood. As was usual at that time, the roof was covered with split hardwood shingles, spiked to wide battens, but these were later protected by corrugated iron.

In 1883, J. T. M. Bell acquired 22,000 acres at Mount Alford, and became the first owner of the property now known as Coochin-Coochin. The old house was transported in sections by bullock waggon, and re-established on high land overlooking a magnificent panorama of mountains and a lagoon. A detached kitchen wing was added, connected to the house by a covered way, and more bedrooms were added to accommodate an increasing family. In 1890, another wing was built, containing a billiard room, school-room, and guest rooms. Another building, for staff quarters and stores, completed the enclosure of a rear courtyard.

"Coochin Coochin" Homestead — Mount Alford

"Nindooinbah" Homestead — Beaudesert   Jopson 68.

The result could have inspired Henry Handel Richardson
when she wrote of "One of those characteristically Australian
houses which, added to wherever feasible, without a thought
for a symmetry of design, a room built on here, a covered
passage there, a bathroom thrown out in an unexpected
corner with odd steps up and down, yet have a spacious,
straggling comfort all of their own."

Coochin is the aboriginal word for black swan, and a
family tradition is that whenever the homestead is occupied
a flag with two black swans on a crimson ground should fly
from a mast at the crest of the hill. The house has entertained
many famous guests, and the garden has trees and palms
planted by members of royal and vice-regal families.

In the era in which it was customary to build such rambling homes, the first holiday-makers began arriving at Southport. Some of them were graziers from the western plains, who brought their families to the seaside to escape the summer heat of the inland. Accustomed to their spacious homesteads, they built equally spacious summer residences along the Esplanade.

Most of them went up towards the end of the century, when labour and materials were cheap. Like most of the buildings in that area, their timber came from Lather's

The Southport School

sawmill, which was established in 1874 on the banks of Gardener's Creek. This flows into the Nerang near its mouth, and was conveniently situated for handling the timber which was floated down to the Broadwater. Great logs of cedar, pine, and beech, cut down with the reckless abandon which was denuding the mountainsides, were fed into the screaming saws, but on Sundays their steel song was replaced by the hymns of Southport residents, who used the mill for religious services.

The Governors of Queensland also had a summer residence at Southport, in a house built near the sawmill by Mr Henry Biggs. When it was no longer used for this purpose, the Rector of Southport realized that it was the perfect site for a boarding school. He was the Reverend H. H. Dixon, later to become Bishop-Coadjutor of Brisbane, and with the aid of friends he acquired the property in 1901. The school opened with six boarders and three day-boys, but enrolments grew rapidly when the same graziers who favoured Southport as a holiday resort realized that it was ideal for the education of their sons.

Naturally enough, it was known as "Dixon's School," but in 1913 it came under the administration of the Church of England, and was re-named The Southport School. The inadequate timber buildings used as the Senior School were replaced by an impressive red-brick structure in the early 1920s, soon after the War Memorial Chapel had been built by public subscription. The Library wing was added in 1954, as a memorial to old boys who had served in the second world war—during which the school was used as a U.S. Army hospital. The old vice-regal quarters are still in use as the Junior School, and the whole complex is now the largest Queensland boarding school for boys.

PRESERVING A HERITAGE

To the early settlers, it must have seemed that the enormous natural resources of the land could never be exhausted. When people realized that nature's balance could not be upset without spilling its wealth as well, it was often too late. The cedar-getters were a good example.

Luckily, there are always those who strive to keep something of our natural heritage for those to whom it will give a different kind of wealth; the refreshment of body and mind. The Hon. R. M. Collins, son of the pioneer William Collins, was one of these.

In 1878 he visited California, where the world's first national parks were being dedicated "for the benefit and enjoyment of the people." This gave him a vision which fired him when he was elected to the Queensland Legislative Assembly and became President of the Royal Geographical Society of Queensland.

The State had no way of preserving land as a national park, but he began a campaign to prevent the despoiling of the McPherson Ranges and to conserve their beauty for the public good. Opposition from the timber interests delayed the passage of an Act until 1907. In 1908, 324 acres of Crown land on the western slope of Mount Tamborine, overlooking the Collins property of Tamrookum, was proclaimed the first National Park. This was followed by a total of 7,220 acres of mountain country surrounding Cunningham's Gap.

R. M. Collins died in 1913, but his long crusade for the protection of the McPherson Ranges was continued by an unlikely aspirant—a descendant of the pioneers of the Canungra timber industry. This was Romeo Lahey, a determined and dedicated engineering student. Even though

Natural Arch
Nerang Valley

Jopson 68.

95

his family was connected with one of the largest timber firms, he was appalled by the destruction and waste of timber in the rain forests. He presented well-reasoned submissions to the local councils, and arranged a public petition to the Minister of Lands. This advocated the reservation of 52,000 acres around the headwaters of the Nerang and Coomera rivers and nearby creeks.

The long fight was won in July 1915, when 47,000 acres were gazetted as the Lamington National Park. Crown land was withdrawn from selection, and the plundering of the mountains had at last come to an end.

The unique wildlife and vegetation are now preserved as a national heritage, and wanderers in the parks can still see the patriarchs of the ranges: the ancient antarctic beeches. These trees, estimated to be over 3,000 years old, are found in only a few widely separated rain forests in the southern hemisphere, but a stand of them is easily accessible from Springbrook. Another prehistoric survivor is the macrozamia palm, to be seen on Mount Tamborine. Clumps of the slender piccabeens also grow densely on these slopes.

Even the casual visitor to the National Parks, who wanders through them along the well-graded walking tracks, can absorb something of the atmosphere of this country as it was before the white man came. The massive trees seem to have fed deeply upon some hidden reservoir of fertility, and tower majestically towards the sun. Their big, glossy leaves are like a living roof of green, filtering the sunlight into a gold-green light which shimmers into mysterious distances. Their branches are festooned with flowering vines and tree-gardens of ferns and orchids.

Giant figs, carribins, and stinging trees are quite common, and if the visitor explores far enough into the more remote areas he may chance upon a red cedar, standing as a solitary monument to the days before these magnificent trees were cut down in their thousands. In the depths of the parks, standing in the dense green silence and looking into the tangle of jungle, one may marvel at the efforts of such men as the two surveyors Roberts and Rowlands, who in 1863 penetrated the mountain ridges and forests to define a border between

Traveller's Palm

Jopson

Macrozamia Palms

Antarctic Beech

97

the new State of Queensland and its parent State of New South Wales.

More recently, other men made an even mightier effort to establish a resort where nature-lovers might live amongst the ranges. In 1912, the eight O'Reilly cousins came from the Blue Mountains, where they had decided that the family grazing properties could no longer support them, to take up eight blocks sprawled across the uninhabited Roberts Plateau, in the heart of the McPherson Ranges. The only way to reach it was by sixteen miles of bridle paths through the great cliffs around the plateau, and by this dangerous route they took in over a thousand tons of supplies, tools, and equipment. Men and packhorses carried 13,528 loads, in order to clear the dense jungle and establish their farms.

Soon after they took up their selection, the Government proclaimed the area as a National Park. No more settlement was to be allowed, so the Reillys' hopes of an access road to the plateau began to fade. Without such a road it would be hard to send out the produce of the farms, so Tom O'Reilly decided to abandon dairy farming and build a small guesthouse on top of the range. The rough road to the bottom of Stockyard Creek Gorge, and the packhorse tracks into the mountains, had to be improved, and sawmilling machinery to build the house had to be hauled up a 3,000-foot mountainside.

Prawners—Southport

Jopson 68

99

The guest-house was opened in 1925, and earned a modest living for the O'Reillys. One of them, Bernard, became nationally known in 1937, when with consummate bushcraft he found and rescued the survivors of an airliner which crashed in the mountains during a cyclone.

One of the earliest visitors to the guest-house was Arthur Groom, who came from the lonely cattle-runs of Central Australia. Fascinated by the contrast which the jungle-clad mountains made to the arid inland plains, he never returned home from the first holiday of his life. He met Romeo Lahey, and with him explored the gorges, waterfalls, and forests. The idea grew between them of establishing another resort, and they decided that a perfect site for it would be on a remote property rising from the southern end of the lush Beechmont farmland. It had magnificent views over the ranges sloping down to the Gold Coast, and in 1933 they floated a public company to acquire 178 acres. They named it Binna-Burra, which in the aboriginal tongue means The Place of the Beech Trees.

After a difficult beginning in the depression years, Binna-Burra grew in popularity. More accommodation was added along the rim of the slope round the levelled area, near the original buildings which have walls of broad-axed hardwood slabs and roofs of split shingles. This original style of construction has been maintained for the newer buildings, relieved by panels of local fieldstone, and the weathered buildings blend perfectly with their site.

Both Bernard O'Reilly and Arthur Groom have described their mountain domains, and their struggles to establish the resorts, in books which tell the story to their visitors.

The ocean which one may glimpse from Binna-Burra Lodge breaks on the seaward shores of Bribie, Moreton, and Stradbroke Islands, which protect the sheltered waters of Moreton Bay. There are 113 islands in the Bay, most of them concentrated to the north of the Broadwater at Southport. The Broadwater, which is now a playground for thousands of craft, has a colourful commercial history.

Among the "worthy mechanics and virtuous migrants" who followed Dr Dunmore Lang's call to emigrate was

Dr Hobbs, who was one of Brisbane's earliest doctors and, as a sideline, decided to harvest the Bay waters. In those days, its waters were home for herds of dugong, the mammal which is also known as the manatee or sea-cow, and which has inspired the legend of the mermaid. Dr Hobbs established a boiling-down works on St Helena Island, and the dugong herds passed through them to emerge as medicinal oil. Like the red cedars, the dugongs are now rarely seen on the Gold Coast, but there have been recent reports of the sighting of small groups.

Oysters grew prolifically in the sheltered waters, but in 1898 the ocean broke through at Jumpinpin, and buried the oyster-beds under silt from the mangrove-swamps along the shore. Today, only a few leases remain, around Currigee. The same ocean breakthrough stopped the practice of swimming mobs of cattle from Labrador to Stradbroke Island. Brought over at low tide, they were driven through the scrub and along the ocean beach to Point Lookout, there to be slaughtered to provide meat for the prison on St Helena Island and the Quarantine Station at Dunwich.

Jopson

Binna Burra Lodge — Beechmont

Whaling from the Bay was continued sporadically until as late as 1959, when the whaling station at Tangalooma was converted into a tourist resort. The whaling fleet has been replaced by craft which hunt at the other extreme of the ocean scale, using nets instead of harpoons but making catches which may be equally profitable. These are the ocean-going prawners, who use the Broadwater as a base and bring back the plump crustaceans which Gold Coast visitors devour in their thousands.

Coral is dredged from the bottom of the Bay, to provide lime for Brisbane's cement-works, and heavy-metals mining is transforming large tracts of Stradbroke Island, but the people of the Gold Coast have begun to realize that the Bay and its islands form a heritage which, at its lowest reckoning, must be preserved if it is to attract holiday-makers. The exploitation of the past has almost denuded the coastline of its natural vegetation, but casuarinas, pines, and pandanus are being grown in Council nurseries to restore the beauty of the foreshores. Now, there is a tendency to look very hard at any projects which may do further damage to the Bay.

Jopson

The most important heritage of any community is its youth, and the Gold Coast area has a fine example of practical care for underprivileged youngsters. This is at Boys' Town, near Beaudesert. The present Parish of St Mary, Beaudesert, is the central district of the Mission of the Logan, which was created in 1874 and whose peripatetic priests ministered to the scattered settlements between Mount Alford, Cleveland, and Tallebudgera. Monsignor Owen Steele, M.B.E., was appointed Parish Priest of Beaudesert in 1943, and during his pastorate conceived the idea of establishing an institution modelled on the famous Boys' Town of Nebraska, U.S.A.

Suitable premises were found in 1960, when the historic home of Mrs T. F. Plunkett, near Beaudesert, and some adjoining properties, were purchased by Sir James Duhig, the Archbishop of Brisbane. Sir James invited the Order of De La Salle Brothers, which is experienced in social work, to establish the new Boys' Town for homeless, neglected, or wayward boys of all races and creeds. Strong support came from the Queensland Government and other religious denominations.

From a modest enrolment of twelve boys in 1961, the number has grown steadily under the guidance of the

Boy's Town Chapel — Beaudesert

Director, Brother Alban, who has enhanced a reputation for energy and zeal. Boys' Town is the only institution in Queensland which educates underprivileged boys to high school level.

As the number of admissions grew, so did the buildings. Attractive brick dormitories, classrooms, and administration blocks have been built to conform with the master plan designed by Shane Ryan. Poultry, pig, and dairy farms have been established, so that Boys' Town is partly self-supporting. On the highest point of the property, a memorial chapel has been built. In modified Romanesque style, it has a slender campanile which has become a local landmark and signifies the fulfilment of a cherished ambition.

Another church, not far from Boys' Town, recalls another man who worked to preserve the heritage of the Gold Coast area. This is All Saints' Church, Tamrookum, erected to the memory of R. M. Collins, who was the moving force

Methodist Church — Southport   Jopson 68.

behind the creation of the National Parks. After his death in 1913, his widow and children followed a family tradition when they decided to build a memorial church beside his grave on Tamrookum, his property south of Beaudesert. The architect was Robin Dods, and he chose local timbers for this fine building. The framing and external walls are of dark stained hardwood relieved by white arches, and the massive pillars and beams supporting the roof are of bluegum. Stained glass windows designed by Sir Richard Lorimer allow a mellow light to rest on the interior linings and furniture which, appropriately to the memory of the man who fought to preserve the ancient timbers of the rain forests, are of red cedar.

Collin's Memorial Church — Tamrookum   Jopson 68.

THE GOLDEN TIDE

The wheel of fortune has turned full circle. When the first settlers cut clearings in the forests behind the Gold Coast, they brought little with them. The land itself was to make them rich. Now, the wealth flows into the land, in a golden tide from many parts of Australia. It is brought in by holiday-makers who are eager to leave their money behind them, avid for diversion and entertainment, seeking at least a glimpse of some way of life which will illuminate the suburbs and country towns to which they return.

They are catered for by a vast variety of entertainments; most of them backed by a sincere desire to give worthwhile value for money, others inspired by a tawdry greed to harvest the tourist dollar. It is interesting to speculate on Lieutenant Cook's reactions if he could now see the lonely coast which he sighted two centuries ago, and wander in his weather-stained blue coat among the crowds which keep the cash-registers playing a merry song.

Three of the most popular attractions developed out of their founders' genuine interest in the subjects which draw thousands of people to see them every year. These are Gilltrap's Auto Museum, the bird and animal sanctuaries at Currumbin and West Burleigh, and the porpoise pools.

George Gilltrap came to the Gold Coast from New Zealand, where he had built up a flourishing earthmoving and farm machinery business. His fascination with the story of transition from animal to mechanical power led him to buy an old Stanley Steam Car, and from this 1939 purchase his collection of veteran cars grew into a small museum.

Public interest was so great that he received many tips on where to buy further acquisitions, and his hobby of finding

1907 Cadillac

1904 Darracq

1914 Detroit Electric

1911 Hupmobile

1902 Albion

1909 Ford "T"

1903 Panhard Levassor

1908 Vulcan

Jopson 68.

107

and restoring old vehicles became so absorbing that it gradually replaced his original business. The collection grew into a range which demonstrates many important steps in the history of transport, and now includes not only veteran and vintage cars but locomotives, tractors, and the world's most famous veteran car: the 1904 Darracq which starred in the film *Genevieve*.

George Gilltrap was persuaded by Queensland's Minister of Tourism to move his collection from New Zealand to the Gold Coast, and established it at Kirra in 1959. The number of exhibits continues to grow, including a Cobb & Co. coach which used to bounce over Queensland roads, and every vehicle has been restored to mint condition and full running order. Their glittering brass and paintwork often add colour to local functions and charity drives.

Mr Gilltrap died in 1966, but his family continues to operate and extend the museum. It has become one of the Gold Coast's best-known and most attractive features.

Between the ocean beach and Currumbin Creek, there is a beautiful headland which has somehow escaped the developers' bulldozers. Beside a quiet lagoon at its foot, Mr Alex Griffiths established an apiary and commercial flower garden in 1947.

The main threat to his success came from the local bird population, which had such an insatiable appetite for nectar that they destroyed his prize blooms. Being a bird lover, he chose to divert them from the flowers with bread soaked in honey, and the news must have spread through the bushland. At morning and evening feeding times, the hungry birds gathered in their screeching, twittering thousands.

The early birds were green and rainbow lorikeets, but these have been joined by many other species. They have become so fearless that they swoop down to eat from plates of food held out by visitors, and even perch on arms and shoulders to await their turn. Not many visitors miss taking part in this phenomenon, and every year the birds feast on 18,250 loaves and 36,500 pounds of honey. The lagoon is now a wildfowl sanctuary, and peacocks, emus, kangaroos and wallabies roam around its shores. An extension into neigh-

Aviary—Currumbin Sanctuary

bouring bushland is planned, to make more space for the more than half-a-million visitors who come each year to feed the birds, buy gemstones in the shop, and gaze into the aviaries and aquaria.

At the West Burleigh Sanctuary, one of the favourite foods is worms. They are eaten by the platypuses which are the principal study of Mr David Fleay, who left the native fauna sanctuary at Healesville, Victoria, in 1957, and acquired fifty acres of scrub country at West Burleigh. He is a zoologist, and the main purpose of his move was to enable him to continue his research into Australian animals, but his Fauna Reserve is open to the public. The platypuses, which not long after Cook's voyage in the *Endeavour* were believed by English scientists to be a practical joke, are one of the most popular features in Mr Fleay's reserve.

Performing Dolphins – Marineland

Platypuses were amongst the many natural species which early exploitation almost rendered extinct. Another was whales, though it is not so long ago that battles between whales and sharks were quite often seen off the Gold Coast beaches. The commercial slaughter of whales became so great that the Moreton Bay whaling station was forced to close down, and the jets of vapour from migrating whales are now a rare phenomenon. But schools of porpoises still gambol in the surf, and occasionally one of them is trapped in the fishermen's nets.

Two bottle-nosed porpoises were shown in the small aquarium opened by Jack Evans in 1957 as an addition to his seawater swimming pool at Point Danger. The former surf champion, who represented Queensland eight times in Australian surf championships, and introduced shark meshing to Queensland beaches, became fascinated with these mammals. Before long, he found himself spending more time with them than he did with humans, and soon realized their potential as a tourist attraction.

After capturing more porpoises, he went overseas to study training techniques and the construction of suitable pools.

In 1962 he established his Porpoise Pool on the Tweed River, and the porpoises leap from its green waters to snatch fish from the hands of bikini-clad beauties.

An extensive Marineland has also been established on the Spit at Main Beach, on eleven acres of sand dunes. Here, experts from American oceanaria have trained a pilot whale and dolphins in tricks ranging from polo-playing to jumping through a hoop of fire. Both companies run a daily marine circus, featuring such events as the hand-feeding of maneating sharks by skin divers, and they have observation windows into their great aquarium pools. Visitors can stare through them at the sharks, turtles, and Pacific Ocean fishes, and the marine creatures can goggle back at the visitors— perhaps with an equally wild surmise.

The development of such attractions, and of the Gold Coast in general, has not been without its critics. "It is not even a Surface Paradise! It is Coney-Island-on-the-Swamps!" was a comment made by one visiting professor when a Planners' Convention was held at Surfers' Paradise, at the height of its development boom.

The Coney Island atmosphere still raises its spangled head, but the dairy farms and wetlands west of the Pacific

Whale Pool & Restaurant
Marineland—Main Beach

Highway were becoming too valuable to leave to cows and mangroves. A bold master plan was drawn up to cover the area from Southport to Broadbeach, but the Albert Shire Council would not approve it without thorough research. This was carried out by the State Harbours and Marine Department and the University of Queensland, who reported that scale model demonstrations showed the risk of flooding to be negligible. On their decision that the scheme was feasible, the construction began.

Millions of cubic yards of earth were dredged out to form artificial bays and inlets. The earth, with sand pumped from the ocean bottom, was used to raise the level of reclaimed land above the highest recorded flood level. Hundreds of building blocks, some with frontages to waterways deep enough to float a fifty-foot craft, became available.

Each of the estates has been planned with its own facilities such as playing fields and shopping centres, and the sealed roads are lined with trees and flowering shrubs. The creation of these waterways developments has now become so widely accepted that a plan is being made to run a canal from the

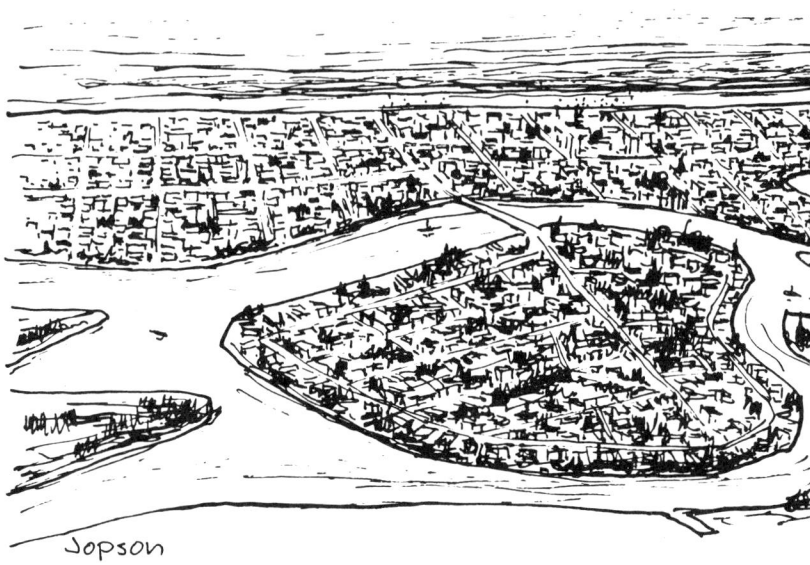

Jopson

keys west of Broadbeach to the Tweed River.

The placid waters of the Gold Coast rivers, especially the Nerang, now echo to the roar of high-powered outboards towing water-skiers, and the Nerang is host to schools which teach this tumultuous sport. It is attracting almost as many devotees as surfing, which was ardently practised along the Queensland coast while Victoria was still on the throne. There was no mystique attached to it then; no jargon about "hanging five" or "wiping out," and no rescue service for the surfer who got into difficulties. Queensland's first life-saving club was formed at Coolangatta, whose name comes from a schooner wrecked there in 1846, when a visiting team from Bondi demonstrated the new techniques with reel and line. This was in 1909, and the movement spread northwards up the surfing beaches. The Southport Club followed in 1913, Kirra in 1916, and Burleigh Heads in 1918.

Soon after the first world war, the Queensland Surf Bathing Association was formed and linked the various clubs together. The first surf clubhouses were built by the enthusiasts with their own hands, and the Surfer's Paradise

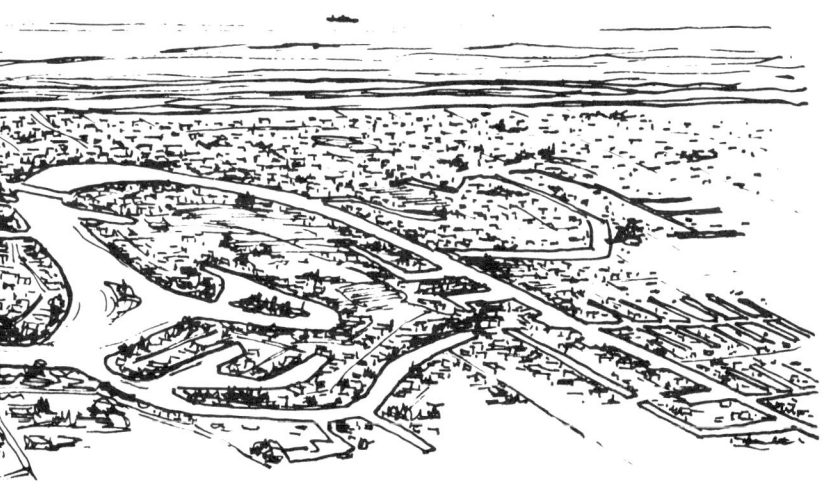

Gold Coast Canal Development

clubhouse was built in this way in 1926. The old buildings seem rather primitive by comparison with the premises now financed by public subscriptions and municipal donations, with rescue equipment donated by large companies, but perhaps the club members do not have any more fun than the "oldies" who rode the surf on their heavy cedar boards.

The Surfers' Paradise Surf Life Saving Club won the first surf-boat race held on the Gold Coast, with a boat presented to them in 1932 by way of a reward for six years of beach patrolling. Now, the various clubs are affiliated with the National Council, and the first Australian Surf Championships were, appropriately, held on Coolangatta Beach.

The first visitors to Surfers' Paradise knew it as Umbigumbi, the Place of the Ant. They were the Aborigines who went to the banksia and ti-tree covered wilderness along the ocean beach for a change in diet, and initiation ceremonies at the ancient bora rings beaten out of the dunes.

The pioneer settler was H. C. Meyer, who established a sugar plantation and cane-crushing mill near the Nerang River. Sugar profits lost their sweetness during the next ten years, so in 1888 he built the Main Beach Hotel, opposite the present site of the Surfers' Paradise Hotel. The area was

New Surf Clubhouse — Bilinga

Jopson

Early Surf Club — Elephant Rock

then known as Elston, and Mr Meyer's hotel was not much
more successful than his sugar plantation. It was burnt down
in 1893, rebuilt in Ferry Road, and served to accommodate
the trickle of holidaymakers. In 1923, Elston was visited by
James Cavill, the owner of two hotels and a sports store in
Brisbane. He found a post office and a few beach shacks
scattered amongst the scrub, and decided that it would be
an ideal place for a fisherman's hotel — in which, in due
course, he could spend his retirement.

A block of land big enough for his hotel cost him only £40,
and he built a "half-timbered" mock-Tudor structure with
sixteen bedrooms. But he found that his guests were attracted
by the surfing instead of the fishing, and that the 1925
opening of the Jubilee Bridge was stimulating interest in
Elston. The area developed rapidly, and, with his true
public relations flair, he re-named it Surfers' Paradise in
1933.

Jim Cavill's hotel, like Meyer's, was burnt down, but
when he rebuilt it in the late 1930's he realized that the time
was ripe for a more ambitious hostelry. He had become an
ardent booster for the area, and built a luxury hotel to
which, with a showman's instinct, he added a private zoo
set in a tropical garden.

During the war his hotel became a convalescent home for
servicemen, and when hostilities ended the golden tide
began. Visitors flocked to Surfers' Paradise, and when James
Cavill died at the age of ninety his dream had been realized.

He had played a part in founding Australia's largest tourist empire of sun, surf, and sand, now more famous for gold than for ants.

The building of the hotel stimulated such interest in Surfers' Paradise that the pre-war holiday shacks fell out of fashion. Usually these had followed the same pattern as the Queensland country houses of the time, with a central core containing kitchen, bedrooms, and living-room, and a veranda on all four sides onto which the visitors' beds overflowed. Set on high stumps to raise the floor above the dunes or foreshore scrub, they had ample space beneath them for car, boat, laundry, shower, and fishing gear. Cheaply constructed of timber, stained black with sump-oil, and corrugated iron roofs, they had few pretensions to comfort. Meals were prepared on a wood stove in the "stove recess," a hot galvanized iron box hung on the external wall. At the end of the garden path, a privy nestled among the banksias.

Such simple shacks were not good enough for the families who now bought land at Surfers' Paradise—for considerably more than the £40 which Jim Cavill had paid for his block. They commissioned architects to design their beach-houses, and these demonstrated the confused styles of the immediate pre-war period. They wore many garbs, including Tudor with steep half-timbered gables, Spanish Mission, log-cabins, and "ship-style" punctured with portholes.

The post-war restrictions on the building of holiday homes caused a lull in the Coast's development, but the brakes came off when the building controls were removed in 1952.

Throughout Australia and in many places overseas, the enormous tourist potential of the Gold Coast became a glittering prize. Land speculation boomed, and families who had bought blocks cheaply in the early days were offered thousands of pounds. Land became too expensive for mere holiday houses, and the soaring values gave impetus to the coastal resorts south of the "mad mile" and to the development of new residential areas along the canals and artificial keys; created out of the swamps and farmlands.

The immediate result was a chaotic outburst of ostentation and vulgarity. Houses, motels, and flats seemed to compete

SURFERS PARADISE HOTEL

BAR

Jopson

Jim Cavill's Hotel — Surfers' Paradise

117

Hotel at Upper Coomera

with each other, as though to see which could become the most vulgar and "modernistic." There were skillion roofs and butterfly roofs, leaning walls and leaning posts, sunburst balustrading and "feature" walls—all in garish and uninhibited colours. Even cypress pine and waterworn stones were varnished, as though to improve upon nature.

Amongst this supermarket proliferation of catchpenny packaging, a group of architectural firms contributed thoughtful houses which are well-suited to the climate, with designs which stand out by their elegance or relaxed simplicity.

But the bubble would not burst. Land values rose until the purchase of land for a holiday home was denied to all but a few. In fact, many of the existing holiday homes were sold at massive profits to the promoters of tower-block apartments, which continue to sprout from Southport to Tweed Heads. Disenchanted by maintaining two houses and two gardens, many week-end residents were glad to sell out, and avail themselves of an apartment held under the strata titles which were introduced in 1960.

But the high-density apartment buildings cast long shadows on the surf beaches, and their traffic is choking the shopping and recreation facilities. Holidaymakers, coming to the Gold Coast for entertainment and relaxation, are finding that the crowds and traffic are worse than they are at home. Town planners, trying to solve the problems of a community which was unprepared for such rapid growth,

Restaurant—Broadbeach

Jopson 68.

are advocating a return to pedestrian shopping precincts and satellite cottage colonies.

Motels, caravan parks, guest-houses and restaurants have spread in ribbon development from Southport to Tweed Heads, many of them built with both eyes on profit and nothing to spare for the overall picture of the area. Though some hotels and apartment tower blocks are well designed, and have a certain appeal.

Some of the district's most progressive pioneers realized that this well-endowed land, with its natural wealth of surf beaches, waterways, and mountains, must be a future holiday resort. One of the earliest innkeepers was Thomas Hanlon, who built the Ferry Hotel at Yatala to serve the staging coaches and river steamers. To be nearer the beaches, he later moved to the infant township of Southport, and opened the first Pacific Hotel on the Esplanade in 1875.

By the time of James Cavill's death, Surfers' Paradise had become a centre for conventions and trade promotions. The new owners of his hotel built the Chevron Hotel, between the highway and the river, and Lennon's acquired a large area at Broadbeach. On this land rose a hotel to accommodate 300 guests.

Both these projects did a great deal to restore parts of the ravaged foreshores. Set in landscaped grounds, they are well-designed along the lines of international resort hotels,

Nerang River Bridge — Broadwater

Jopson

with swimming pools, beer gardens, and facilities for conventions and entertainments.

The new owners of the Upper Coomera Hotel also did their part in restoring something of that which was almost forgotten. Using bush timber, waterworn stones, and bark roofing, they have rebuilt the hotel in the district's pioneer tradition.

One of the early hotel-keepers was a man who played a part in opening up Gold Coast communications. He was P. J. Fagan, who built the railway stations between Nerang and Coolangatta, and then settled on the knoll overlooking Rainbow Bay and the surf beach. There, in 1903, he opened the first section of the Greenmount Guesthouse, and in 1908 he was the first man permitted to drive a motor-car through the border fence between Queensland and New South Wales. His chugging engine heralded the slow demise of the railway which he helped to build, because cars and road transport have made the South Coast line so unprofitable that it had to be closed down.

Millions of sun-seeking southerners have passed through the border fence since P. J. Fagan's day, in a weight of traffic which forced the rebuilding of the Nerang Bridge. For forty years, its timber span had done its part in helping the development of the thirty miles of holiday resorts from Southport to the Tweed, but the sinking piles and undulating deck could no longer stand the strain. In 1966, a splendid four-lane concrete bridge, designed and built by the Main Roads Commission of Queensland, began to cope with the endless cavalcades of coaches, buses, trucks, semi-trailers and cars.

Before either of the bridges was built, there was no way for vehicles to travel between Southport and Main Bridge except by ferry. The first one was established by H. C. Meyer to serve his sugar-plantation on the Nerang, and ran until the timber bridge was opened in 1925.

Most of the earlier visitors to the Gold Coast preferred to travel by boat, because the few roads serving the area were no more than rutted tracks. When Cobb & Co began their coach service to the border, they preferred the beaches to the roads, but their thrice-weekly timetables had to coincide

Pond Mining — Sth. Stradbroke Island

Heavy Minerals Dredge
Sth. Stradbroke Island

with low tides at Kirra Heads. Their teams galloped along
the firm sands in fine style from 1884 until the South Coast
railway was extended to Nerang, and then the coach
contracts to cover the gap between the rail terminus and the
Tweed were taken over by the Gaven family. Gaven Way,
the inland road to the Gold Coast through Nerang, is
named after them.

Gold has never been discovered on the Gold Coast—the
name itself being a public relations invention. But far more
useful minerals, to a value which would make the yields of
most gold-strikes seem puny, have been extracted from the
sands of the mainland and the islands. The holidaymakers
who bronze themselves on the Gold Coast beaches may never
have heard of rutile, but it could have been used in building
the aircraft which brought them in to the Gold Coast
airport—one of Australia's busiest outside the State capitals.
Rutile, with zircon, ilmenite, and monazite, are mined along
the beaches, and are in worldwide demand. When a tall
young man began prospecting for them in 1939 the locals
gave him the name of "Mad Murphy," but it is a nickname
now applied with a touch of rueful pride. The strata of black
sand to which he shovelled down at Tweed Heads, near the
tent in which he lived on the beach, have made multi-
millionaires of him and his two brothers.

As with Jim Cavill when he built his hotel, the times were
in his favour. Soon after James Murphy commenced beach-

Minerals Barge & Tug — The Broadwater

mining, the second world war created an insatiable market
for his minerals. His brothers joined him in the infant
industry, and when the war ended the demand increased.
The minerals with their names which seem almost to belong
to science fiction were needed for sophisticated aircraft and
weaponry, and even for space vehicles, as well as for many
appliances used in everyday life.

In the Southport area, various companies began mining
the beaches, foreshores, and sand-dunes on South Stradbroke
Island. Soon, the old battle flared up anew, between those
who would tear wealth from the land and those who bitterly
blamed them for the destruction of the natural beauty of the
area. The leaseholders were obliged to prevent erosion and
rehabilitate the beaches, but when the dredges moved on they
replaced dunes and indigenous vegetation with grassed areas
and monotonous rows of exotic pines.

In 1967, the space vehicle which landed on the moon was
partly built from metals mined on the Gold Coast. The
export earnings of the beach-mining companies, thirty years
after James Murphy sank his shovel into the black sands,
have reached appropriately astronomical proportions. They
hover around thirty-one million dollars a year.

At Hollywell, a water transport terminal provides an
anchorage for the gaily-decorated barges which transport

Panorama Tower

the minerals from the beaches and islands to the Brisbane export wharves, following the same sea-route used by the cedar rafts nearly a century ago.

The beach-miners have not been the only cause of fore-shore erosion. The 1967 cyclone did far greater damage. Protective dunes disappeared, and the sea destroyed stretches of the esplanade and threatened the foundations of some of the multi-storey apartment buildings. To save them, thousands of tons of boulders were excavated from the mountains, and dumped along the surf beaches to form artificial cliffs.

This experience, together with the prohibitive costs of waterfront land, has caused investors to look elsewhere for high-rise home-unit and apartment sites. The first of these to be built away from the waterfront was Panorama Tower, which has been sited on the bank of the Nerang River at Surfers Paradise. Those who dwell in it have panoramic views of ocean, river, and the Nerang farms, with their dramatic background of the McPherson Ranges. The project has proved so popular that others are being built.

These elegant towers are a far cry from the old high-stump buildings which were for so long a characteristic of Queensland. The high-stump erections are slowly being replaced

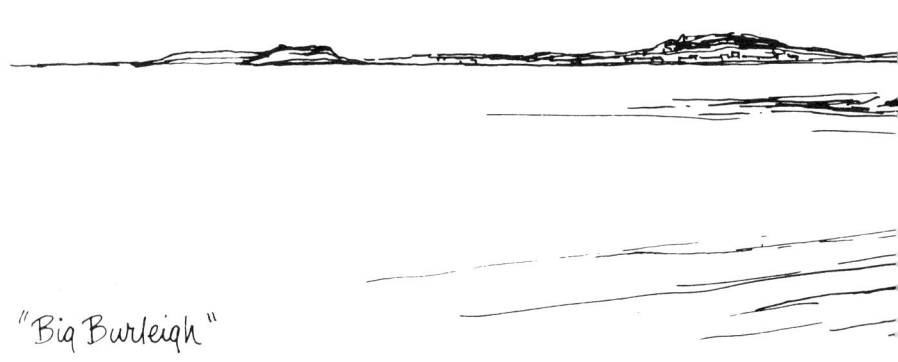

"Big Burleigh"

by more conformist structures, and with them are departing such customs as "stump-capping." When the stumps had been placed for a church, there would be quite a festive gathering, and members of the congregation would step forward to "cap" each of the stumps with a donation.

But it seems that "the more things change, the more they remain the same." Since the transportation of convicts to Moreton Bay was stopped in 1839, the Gold Coast area has poured out its wealth in various ways to various types of people. There have been those who raped the land without a thought for the future, and those who cherished the land for its deeper wealth of peace, contentment, and beauty. Now, perhaps, the balance is about even. The golden tide flows in, and there are plenty to fish in its waters, but for countless folk the Gold Coast represents the good life, in which they can taste the riches of freedom against the ageless background of sun, sand, and sea.

Jopson 68

TROPICAL
QUEENSLAND

Drawings by
AINSLIE ROBERTS

Text by
PETER NEWELL

CONTENTS

Sugar Cane Burn-off

130

SUGAR COUNTRY

"We have mineral wealth incalculable, agricultural land in vast quantities, pastoral country to be reckoned by the hundred square miles, but we cannot avail ourselves of our wealth from the simple fact that we have not men to people our land." So lamented the editor in the *Cooktown Almanac* in 1876, and his words echo to this day. The need to defend and develop our North, with its rapid expansion of mining, industry, and primary production, makes the growth of population an urgent national problem.

In 1855, the Government promised to flood Queensland with cheap labour from India. It proved to be unobtainable, but 170 Javanese were indentured to the Johnston River plantation. They adapted well, but the Dutch authorities discouraged further recruitment.

Captain Robert Towns, after whom Townsville was named, was the first to realise that a more prolific source of labour was closer at hand, and in 1863 he sent his schooner *Don Juan* to the Pacific Islands to recruit "Kanakas" for his cotton plantations. The labourers whom he brought from the New Hebrides were the first of many, and only four years later it was estimated that there were 6,000 "black slaves" in Queensland. Most of them were indentured to planters for ten shillings a month, plus rations, clothing, and shelter.

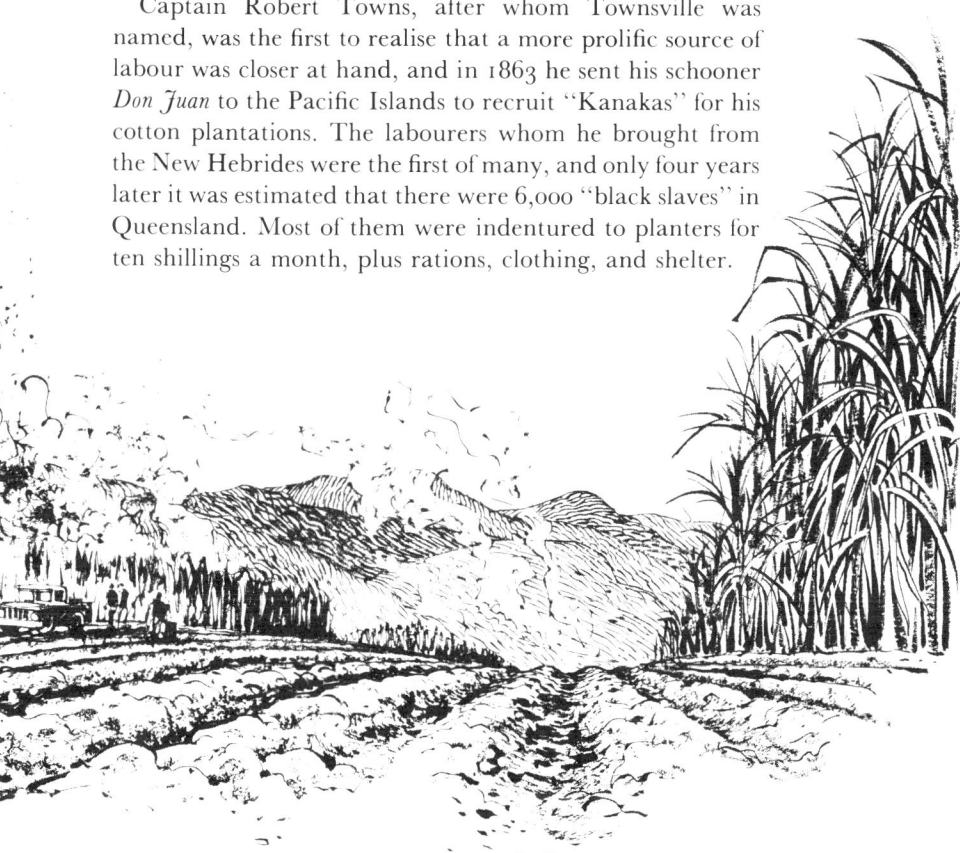

Stories that Captain Towns kidnapped the Kanakas and forced them to work are unfounded. Historians believe that the islanders, at first, were happy to go to a new land and work for a white master, but the demand for labour soon became so strong that the blackbirders had to go further afield, and eventually resorted to guile and bloodshed to lure natives onto their ships. The islanders responded by murdering and eating any white man they could catch.

The trade was condemned by churchmen, island missionaries, and the trade unions, who feared that their hard won working conditions would be undermined by cheap labour. With the assistance of the Royal Navy, the trade was regularised in 1871. Brutality and abuses were brought under control, and "Inspectors of Polynesians" sailed in the recruiting ships. The Queensland authorities insisted that repatriated Polynesians should be issued with western dress, and an eye-witness described a New Hebridean islander, reporting for his free passage home on expiry of his three-year "indenture," as being dressed in a "black Paget coat, riding trousers, and a black bell-topper hat of the latest cut . . . with a pair of lemon coloured kid gloves on his hands, a red necktie and a silver watch and chain. . . ."

Some time-expired Kanakas preferred to sign on for further periods of indenture. A few families remained, and groups of their descendants can be found in some Northern sugar towns. Between 1869 and 1906, when the trade was prohibited, some 60,819 Kanakas were imported under varying conditions of competence and corruption.

Economic factors, as much as political and humane issues, contributed to the decline in the Kanaka system. The cost of importing and maintaining Kanakas was rising, planters were competing for time-expired men, the plough was superseding the hoe, and acclimatised white men were proving to be more productive workers.

Long before then, pioneer graziers starved of labour had introduced Chinese workers into the State to attend the sheep on their unfenced selections. These shepherds or "hut keepers" were being replaced by boundary riders when they suddenly caught gold fever, and deserted their flocks for the

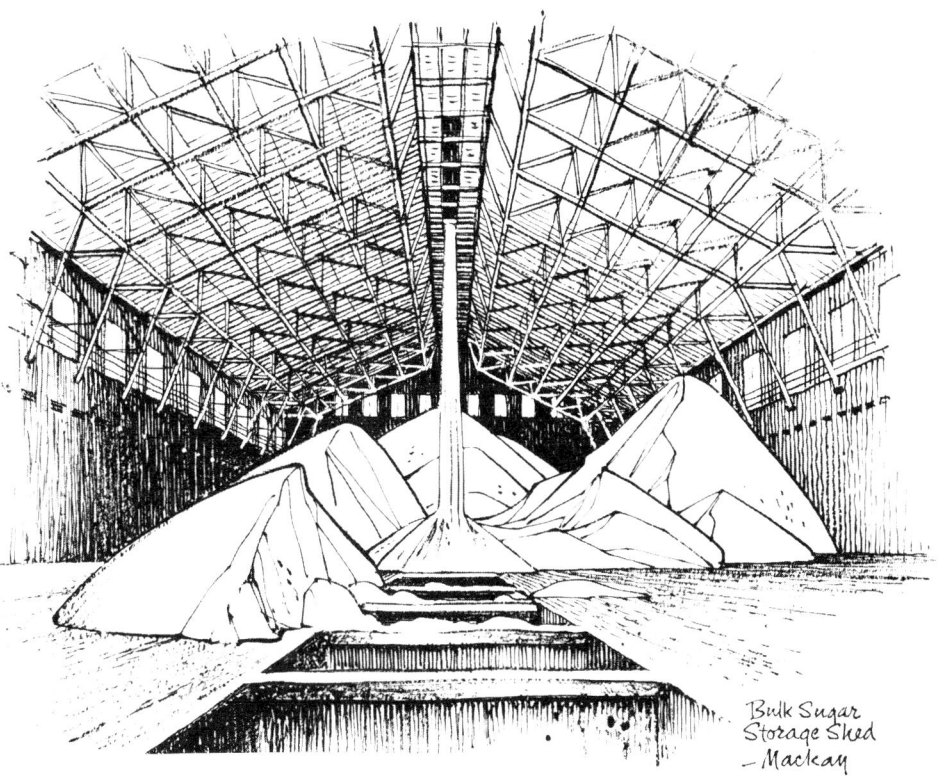

Bulk Sugar
Storage Shed
— Mackay

Northern diggings. They were followed by shiploads of their countrymen, recruited to labour on the Palmer River gold-fields, and by 1877 the Chinese coolies far outnumbered the white miners. Many of them were killed and eaten by the ferocious Cape myalls, who preferred their flavour to the saltier taste of white men. The Chinese were controlled by "tongs," or secret societies, well disciplined by their leaders and their hatchet men, and some bloody feuds over disputed claims broke out between rival tongs.

The increasing number of Chinese, with their insanitary habits and low standard of living which spread the epidemic diseases brought through the inadequate quarantine inspection, caused a public outcry which in 1878 forced the Government to forbid further Asian immigration. In 1890, the Queensland Premier, Sir Samuel Griffith, made the first attempt to check the import of Kanakas and force the repatriation of those working on the plantations, and it was becoming apparent that coloured labour could no longer be relied upon as a cheap source of workers.

The situation was eased temporarily by unsuccessful miners drifting south from the minefields, whose golden years were in decline. No strangers to hard work, and preferring an open air life after years in the pits, they saw an opportunity to end the years spent as "wages men" by acquiring their own farms. But they, and other white Queenslanders, proved insufficient to satisfy the demand for labour, and there was some gloom over the future of the sugar industry.

Then two Italians, Armati and Faire, who had founded successful businesses in Townsville, suggested that their countrymen should be encouraged to migrate as workers for the canefields. C. V. Faire was prepared to back up his vision with action, and with the endorsement of the Chamber of Commerce he visited the farming districts of northern Italy.

He recruited 320 labourers, many of whom brought their families, under terms which bonded them for two years of

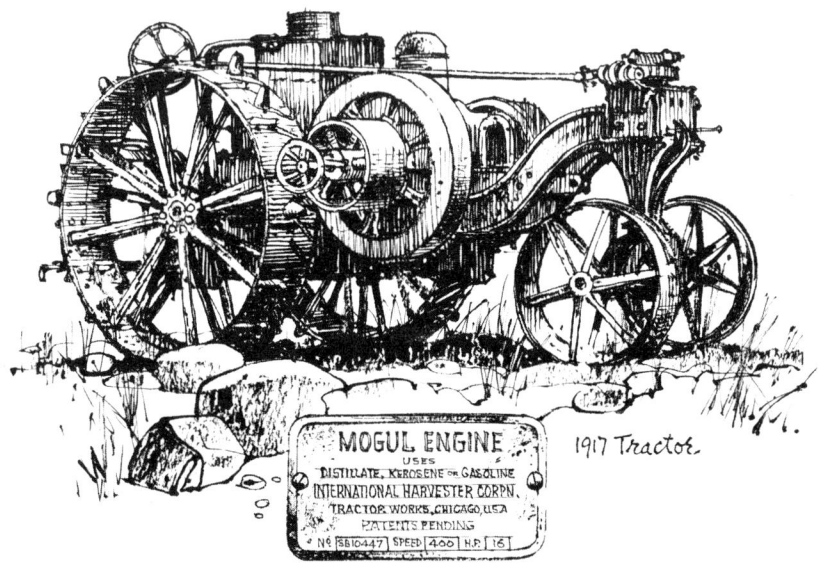

MOGUL ENGINE
USES
DISTILLATE, KEROSENE or GASOLINE
INTERNATIONAL HARVESTER CORPN,
TRACTOR WORKS, CHICAGO, U.S.A.
PATENTS PENDING
Nº 8610447 SPEED 400 H.P. 16

1917 Tractor.

Roadside
Relics

135

canefield labour. After this they were entitled to lease or purchase a farm, with an assured sale of the cane to the local mill. The first Italians disembarked at Townsville in December 1891, and were dismayed at the hostility which they encountered from local working men. Like the Kanakas, and Chinese, they were regarded as possible saboteurs of Australian working conditions.

But they settled down, and soon sent glowing reports to relatives in Italy. The opportunities of which they wrote, together with the restriction of immigration into the U.S.A., set off a flow of Italian migrants which still continues. After the second World War, the expansion in sugar assignments attracted even larger numbers of South Europeans into the cane belt along the coast of tropical Queensland.

For residents of this belt, sugar is not only the basic industry but virtually a way of life. Lovers of this lush, beautiful country have many evocative memories. At harvest time, evening skies are reddened by the burning off of "trash" amongst the cane, to make cutting easier and drive out snakes and vermin. For six months of the year, the rich odour of raw sugar hangs heavily around the thirty-four mills which crush the cane from about 8,700 cane farms in the sugar belt, working the clock round for seven days a week.

The first commercial sugar was cultivated by the Honourable Louis Hope in 1862 on his property near Brisbane. When the North Queensland coastal belt proved to be too hot and wet for sheep, the settlers began planting sugar; firstly at Innisfail in 1880, and soon spreading out through the rich alluvial country and fertile valleys as far north as Cairns. Mills were built to serve each district, and the Victoria Mill near Ingham, now one of the largest in the world, was crushing cane in 1883. Two years later the first processed sugar was exported to London, and since then this huge industry has been organised so efficiently that it can compete on world markets with countries employing low-cost labour.

About half the output is exported, the remainder being used by the world's greatest sugar-eaters—the Australians themselves. Australia is second only to Cuba as a sugar

Cane Train / Diesel.

exporter, and sugar earns more than any other of Queensland's primary industries; both facts proving that a "white
economy" can succeed in the tropics. New techniques are
constantly being introduced throughout the industry, from
fertilising to hauling. The cutter who wields his cane knife
amongst the soot-blackened stalks is rapidly becoming as
outdated as a Kanaka with a hoe, because much of the cane,
now drawn by diesel engines along the 2,000 miles of narrow
gauge railways which link the mills to their "assigned"
farms, is harvested mechanically. Even the sugar-bag is
becoming a museum piece, because sugar is now being
handled like wheat, by bulk loading and sea transport.

Nothing is wasted. The primary by-product, molasses, is
converted into rum, headache powders, and many other
products. The "bagasse," which is the mass of cane-fibre
remaining when the juice has been crushed out, is compressed
into building board. The residual "mud" is a rich fertiliser
which restores the fertility of the canefields, and so the
process begins all over again.

Horseshoe Bay,
BOWEN

BOWEN TO TOWNSVILLE

That aristocratic Scot, George Elphinstone Dalrymple, was
the founder of Bowen and Cardwell and one of Australia's
most extraordinary frontiersmen. Explorer, politician, pastoralist, and inventor, he was the foremost figure in the
expansion of North Queensland between 1869 and 1874, the
period in which he explored the vast coastline between the
Burdekin and Endeavour Rivers and opened up the Kennedy
District for pastoral development.

In 1861, he led an overland expedition from Rockhampton to establish the North's pioneer settlement, while a sea-
borne expedition of settlers with their supplies and livestock
sailed from Brisbane in the Government-chartered schooners
Jeannie Dove and *Santa Barbara*. The captain of the latter

138

had discovered the anchorage of Port Denison in 1859 while searching for a suitable port for the area. In 1861 a township was surveyed and named Bowen, after Sir George Ferguson Bowen, then Governor of Queensland. By 1865 the population was over 1,000.

In August 1862, the infant settlement was visited by John McKinlay's party, at the end of their long trek from Adelaide up to the Gulf Country in search of survivors from the Burke and Wills expedition. After describing the well-watered grazing land which they had traversed after striking eastwards from the Gulf, they reported that the settlement already was "A presentable array of buildings including, of course, public houses, blacksmiths' forges and general stores."

Links with an historic past are everywhere. The Court House, a fine example of Colonial architecture and the first Supreme Court in North Queensland, was opened in 1881 after fifteen years in building. At Strathmore stands the old Bowen River Hotel, much as it was a century ago and a classic example of split-slab bush carpentry. It is preserved as the North's only surviving teamster's hostelry.

Port Denison, the fine natural harbour, is capable of handling a much larger trade, but the choice of Townsville and Mackay as sites for the bulk sugar terminals was a severe setback for Bowen. Nevertheless it handles a wide variety of produce from its rich hinterland, from coal and meat to fruit, vegetables and the famous Bowen mangoes.

Bowen Court House

Introduced from India, these mangoes would not have been amongst the products noted by James Cook, in accordance with his Admiralty instructions to "observe the nature of the soil, its products, beasts, fowls, fishes, minerals, trees, fruits, grains . . . and the genius, temper, disposition, and number of the natives."

In the winter of 1770, Lieut. Cook skilfully sounded his way northwards through the reef-fanged waters of the Coral Sea, and on 6 June the *Endeavour* entered a wide bay dominated by a massive red granite hill, which he named Cleveland Bay. He anchored under the lee of a large island in the bay, and noticed the ship's compass behaving so erratically that he thought erroneously that the island must exert some magnetic influence. He named it Magnetical Island; a name which has survived without its suffix.

Bowen River Hotel
Est. 1873

Magnetic Island
Shoreline,

Scientists from the *Endeavour* collected a few more botanical specimens for Mr Banks, and the bay was left undisturbed until Captain Phillip King sailed the *Mermaid* in there some fifty years later, and spent three days in local surveys.

Another half-century passed, and the pioneering Butler family became the first to settle at Picnic Bay on the island. Before a proper Quarantine Station was built on the mainland, the Butlers inspected the immigrant ships which arrived with the yellow flag requesting medical clearance—an important point in those days when the diseases of the Orient and Occident were being imported into the hitherto unpolluted air of Australia. Ships bearing troops, convicts, or

Townsville
and Castle Hill

immigrants brought with them the germs and viruses of every epidemic disease from malaria to typhoid, of which many were then known under the catch-all phrase of "fever." They devastated the Aborigines and affected every settlement. In 1866, two-thirds of Burketown's residents died, and typhoid alone killed 500 of Townsville's early citizens. Such afflictions fortified the myth that white men could not thrive nor labour in the tropics; a myth that persisted until Dr S. H. Frodsham, the third Bishop of North Queensland, joined the doctors of Townsville General Hospital in a crusade for the first medical research institute in Australia. In 1910, the Institute of Tropical Medicine was opened in an empty storehouse at the Townsville Hospital, headed by the brilliant scientist Dr Anton Breinl. He wrote, "The question of populating a tropical country with a white race has entered a new era . . . free the tropics from disease, and the white man

will thrive there just as well if not better than in a temperate climate." By 1930, when the Institute was moved to Sydney, this contention had been proved.

Proper public health administration and successive native-born generations have produced the world's largest and most successful settlement in the tropics by a community more than ninety-five per cent of European origin. It is intriguing, however, to speculate upon the multiracial population which might have developed in North Queensland but for the White Australia policy, which was strongly supported in the area and a major catch-cry at the time of Federation.

On Magnetic Island, the Butlers were followed by the enterprising Hayles family, which realised its potential, built the first hotel, and began the water transport which opened up island land for fruit farming and holiday resorts. Now, it is virtually an island suburb of Townsville, though most of its twenty-one square miles of rugged and scrub-covered hills was proclaimed a National Park in 1953, to protect its native flora and fauna including rock wallabies and koala bears. Thirty minutes on the ferry link Townsville with the island, with its beautiful bays and pines growing between the massive boulders along the coastline.

Townsville was not only named after Captain Robert Towns, but financed by him. After the separation of Queensland from New South Wales in 1859, liberal land laws were passed to encourage settlers in the North, but the new port of Bowen was too remote for those who took up land round the fine natural harbour of Cleveland Bay. John Melton Black, who managed one of Towns's chain of huge pastoral properties stretching from Bowen to the Gulf country, recommended him to establish a more accessible port, and the first wharf was built on Ross Creek in 1864. A thriving community developed around it, while the partnership of Towns, the self-made Sydney merchant, with the versatile Black literally changed the face of North Queensland.

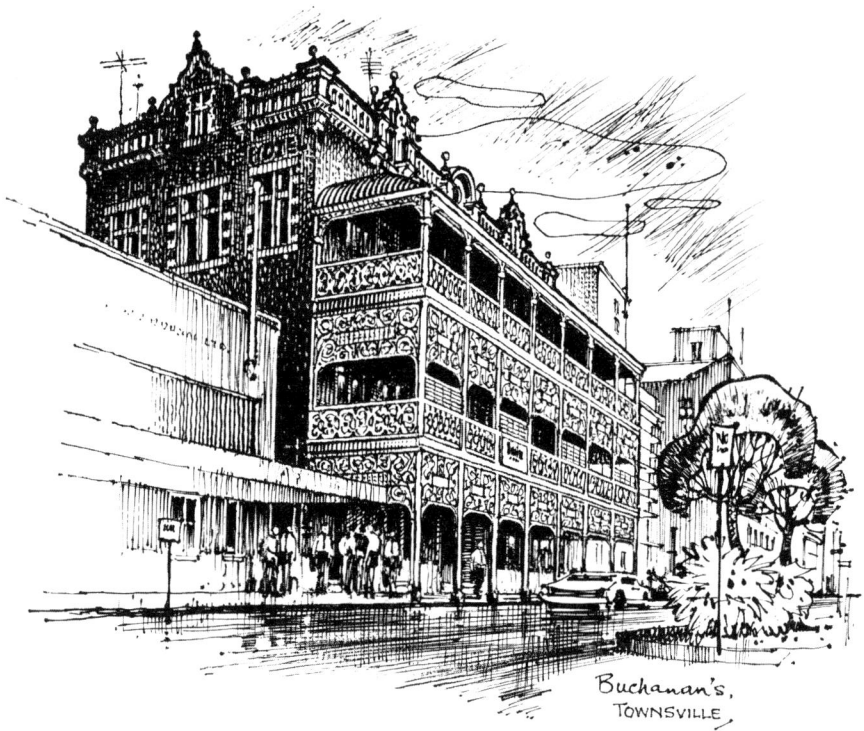

Buchanan's, Townsville

Boat Basin / Burns Philp, TOWNSVILLE

Another partnership with far-reaching consequences was formed when a hardworking, determined Scot named Robert Philp joined the brothers James and John Burns, who opened a general store in Townsville in 1872. The partnership, formed in 1876, rapidly extended their activities through North Queensland into New Guinea and the Pacific Islands. The merchants became shipowners, bought plantations, and founded the Queensland Insurance Company. Today Burns Philp is known throughout the South Pacific, with 10,000 employees and a vitality which is taking it into the hotel and motel field to satisfy the demands of tourism.

By 1870, Townsville had grown into a village of about 700 people, most of whom lived in shacks and tents along the foreshore. A brighter future was promised by the boom in

Anglican Cathedral

mining, sugar, and pastoral interests, and the residents petitioned for the establishment of a Church of England. The Reverend Adams was sent from Sydney, and in 1871 land was bought on Melton Hill and work was begun on the first Church of St James. But in 1878 Dr C. H. Stanton was consecrated as the first Bishop of North Queensland, and commissioned the architect Arthur Blackett to design an appropriate cathedral. Blackett advised building with thick walls of the local red granite and a double roof, to combat the heat.

The foundations were laid, but the boom collapsed. Only a part of Blackett's design was carried out, in red brick instead of stone, and six years later the hall, lined with the rich red cedar then plentiful in North Queensland, was built in the grounds. The 1902 cyclone unroofed the Cathedral, and it was not until 1952 that Ian Shevill, sixth Bishop of North Queensland, completed the building.

146

In 1961, the Premier of Queensland opened the University College of Townsville, then a college of the University of Queensland, in the suburb of Pimlico, and 180 day and evening students were enrolled. Enrolments and departments grew steadily, the Townsville City Council donated 650 acres at the foot of Mount Stuart, and in April 1970 Queen Elizabeth opened what is now the fully independent James Cook University of North Queensland; Australia's first university in the tropics.

The university will be closely integrated with economic and educational developments in the North, and research into problems of relevance to its environment will be emphasised—such as the study of Queensland's precious but threatened natural heritage, the Great Barrier Reef, by the Department of Marine Biology with the aid of a generous Commonwealth grant. South-East Asian studies have been added to the degree courses in arts, science, engineering, commerce, and economics, and a post-graduate School of Tropical Veterinary Science is planned. A residential Teachers' College is being established near by.

Such new developments of tropical Queensland as the James Cook University are in extreme contrast to some almost vanished remnants of the roaring days of a century ago. These include the ghost town of Ravenswood, now disappearing under a jungle of vines and China-apple trees

University Library, Townsville

Residence, Railway Hotel, Old Chimneys..
Ravenswood

to the east of Mingela, a township between Townsville and
Charters Towers, which has more goats than citizens.

The first alluvial gold in the district was found in 1868, by
a stockman on Ravenswood station. Reefs further west were
petering out, and miners who heard that the first month's
crushing at Ravenswood had yielded 2,000 ounces of gold
were quick to abandon what a newspaper described as "the
patience, patchwork, rags, resignation, Chinamen and fleas
of the Cape River." The rush which they joined sent Ravens-

wood's population soaring from a mere handful to 6,000,
served by a railway, gasworks, and forty-two pubs, but in
1872 the mine-shafts began to flood at the seventy-foot level.
Mine after mine was closed down, and the diggers drifted to
the latest Eldorado at Charters Towers, some fifty miles away.
Despite this, Ravenswood took a long time to die. It was kept
going during the 1880s by the extraction of silver and lead,
until the smelting works failed and the town slumped back
into the doldrums. However, there was another revival in

1900, when, with the help of English capital, the New Ravenswood Company was formed, to integrate several of the surviving mines under one experienced manager. Life returned to Macrossan Street and the new company profitably worked the local lodes until finally the mine workings became completely uneconomical in 1920.

Now, the only monuments to the rollicking miners are two red brick chimneys thrusting out of the bush, eroded mullock heaps, and decaying headframes. Two abandoned hotels survive amongst the crumbling foundations and other fragments of once impressive buildings. With their timber verandahs, frosted glass panels, and richly carved red cedar appointments they are typical examples of the hotel architecture of the boom days.

Relics at Ravenswood

Old Stock Exchange.
CHARTERS TOWERS.

"THE WORLD" TO INGHAM

Today, it is hard to believe that Charters Towers was once
the second city of Queensland; so rich and vigorous and
teeming with life that it was affectionately called "The
World" by its proud citizens. During its Golden Age, in the
1890s, the little town which now drowses in the sun had a
population five times larger than that of today, fifty-eight
hotels, eight churches, three newspapers, a stock exchange,
and several theatres. At the railway station, more than fifty
spanking four-in-hand coaches met the trains.

It is nearly a century since Jupiter, an Aboriginal boy with
Hugh Mosman's party of prospectors in the near-by hills,
picked up a piece of gold-bearing quartz. More gold was
found in surface reefs, and Mosman hurried to register his
claim at the Mining Commissioner's office, Ravenswood.

The rush was on, and "The Towers" quickly became Queensland's most famous goldfield. Before the reefs petered out at the turn of the century, gold valued in those days at over £30 million had been produced.

For twenty years or so, Charters Towers lived high. The citizens worked hard and played hard. Saturday night was miner's night, when the pubs and stores along the gas-lit streets were thronged with shoppers and revellers. Bowler-hatted miners in their best flannel shirts and bell-bottomed moleskins escorted women fashionably decked out in bustles and plumes. At each end of Mosman Street there was a brass band, rivalling each other in attempts to drown out the rhythmic pounding of the stampers crushing the seemingly unending procession of dray-loads of gold-bearing quartz.

But the gold did come to an end, and many of the town's houses and other buildings were plucked off their stumps and transported to new settlements as far west as Cloncurry. Other such mining towns as Charters Towers have died when their golden lifeblood ebbed, but "The World" has survived and even flourished in its own quiet way. Luckily, a pastoral industry was growing while the mines were being depleted. In 1885, the Allingham brothers overlanded thousands of sheep from Armidale, New South Wales, to their selection on the Fletcher River, and they were followed by other graziers who took up the surrounding country. Since then, the district has become one of Queensland's most prosperous cattle centres, and the equable climate and loamy soil have been found ideal for growing citrus, tropical fruits, and even grapes. And not far from the many relics of the golden past are to be found the promise of tropical Queensland's future, because Charters Towers has become an educational centre. Its pleasant atmosphere, at 1,000 feet above sea level, has attracted several colleges and boarding schools which draw their students from the far west and north and even from the Pacific Islands.

One of the most eminent of these schools is All Souls', which was opened by the Brotherhood of Saint Barnabas in 1920. The Brotherhood itself has a romantic history.

In the early days of settlement, the churches had great difficulty in obtaining preachers with sufficient dedication to

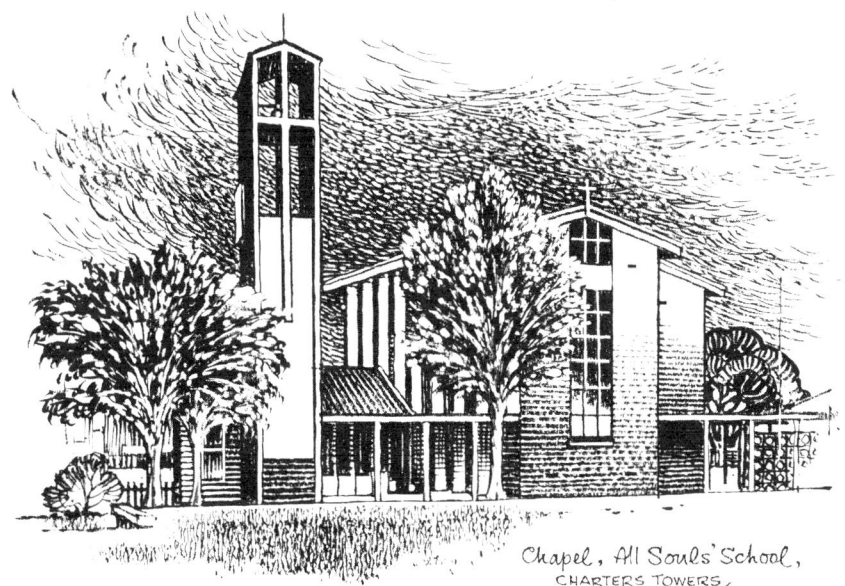

Chapel, All Souls' School, CHARTERS TOWERS

face the loneliness and difficulties of ministering to tiny congregations scattered over 100,000 square miles of remote stations and mining camps. The Reverend Vaughan Williams, who was the thirteenth rector appointed to Herberton in as many years, solved the problem in 1901 by founding the Brotherhood. He sought a "band of men that will preach like apostles, ride like cowboys, and, having food and raiment, will therewith be content." Brothers had to vow celibacy and poverty, and to serve anywhere in the vast diocese for at least five years.

Few Australians offered, so Vaughan recruited men from Oxford and Cambridge universities. The Brothers who now make parish visits by truck or aircraft live more easily than those pioneers, but their sense of dedication is the same. As well as inspiring the foundation of All Souls' School, now the largest boys' private school in the far north of Australia, it created the Community of Saint Barnabas, a permanent teaching order which serves the north.

A similar dedication lies behind the Royal Flying Doctor Service, for which Charters Towers was chosen as a regional

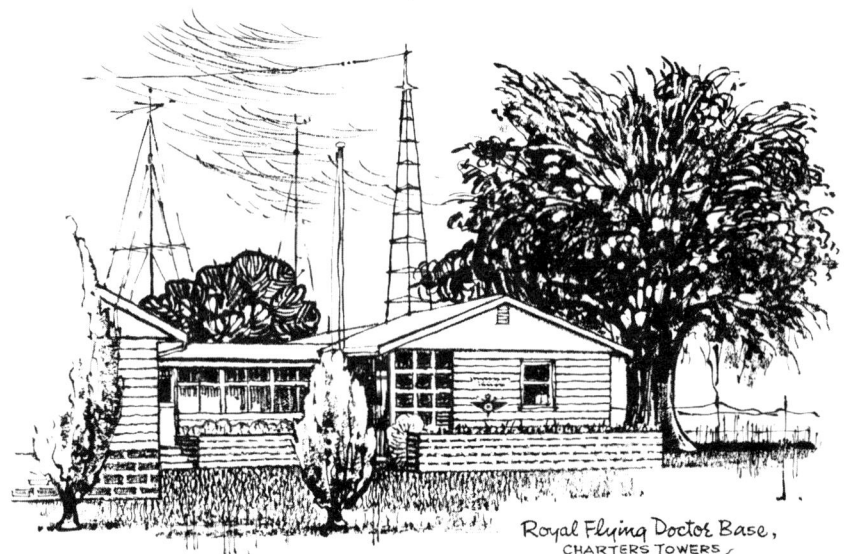

Royal Flying Doctor Base, CHARTERS TOWERS

base during the late 1950s because of its excellent hospital and airfield. The other two Queensland regional bases, which were found necessary to control the increasingly widespread operations of the R.F.D.S., are at Charleville and Mount Isa. The latter was moved there from Cloncurry in 1963, to meet the needs of that mining boom area.

It was at Cloncurry, of course, that the R.F.D.S. began, when the first of the flights inspired by the Reverend John Flynn of the Australian Inland Mission took off in 1927. Since then, the "mantle of safety" which he foresaw has been spread over the outback regions of every State in the Commonwealth, and there have been many side-benefits. The hundreds of radio transceivers installed in remote mining camps, pastoral properties, and police stations have made the Inland articulate, and destroyed the "Great Australian Loneliness" which once afflicted those who had to exist out of touch with their own kind. The unique School of the Air, which keeps outback children in touch with their teachers, relies entirely on Flying Doctor radio links.

In tropical Queensland, the R.F.D.S. is assisted by other aerial services, including the Cairns-based Aerial Ambulance and the Bush Pilots; the local airline which is the friend, carrier, and lifeline of people in the Cape and Gulf country.

North from Charters Towers lies Ingham, in the centre of the lush sugar-cane district along the lower Herbert River. This progressive and well-planned town retains a strong Italian atmosphere from the early migrants; so much so that youths and girls follow the age-old Italian custom of parading in groups in the evening, with banter between the groups flying in the tongue of their pioneering grandparents.

But the town itself is typically Queensland, with houses raised on high stilts. So it is surprising to see, under a roof of richly-textured blue-grey tiles of an unusual pattern, an authentic old Japanese house.

Now occupied by Doctors John and Pamela Markwell, the house must surely be Queensland's first "prefab," because it was imported from Japan by Judge G. W. Paul.

Japanese House, INGHAM

In 1887 he decided to build a house in Brisbane, and remembering the houses he had occupied in Japan he realised that their design was ideal for hot, humid climates. House and craftsmen were brought to Brisbane, and they built so well that it was still standing in 1961, when the property was acquired for flat development. Several architects tried to persuade the Brisbane City Council to buy the house and rebuild it in New Farm Park, as an historic tourist attraction, but eventually it was sold at public auction to the Markwells. A group of architectural students made measured drawings, each component was marked, and the house was dismantled and transported to Ingham, where it was re-assembled by local Italian carpenters. The framing, still sturdy after seventy-four years, and the movable walls, all fitted together perfectly, and the beautifully carved tokonomas and "moon window" are like memorials to the craftsmanship of the Japanese who came to an alien land to build the house.

Hinchinbrook Island
and Channel

Dunk Island
from Moonglow, Mission Beach

157

CATTLEMEN AND CHINAMEN

The botanist and explorer Allan Cunningham returned from his epic journey of exploration through the Darling Downs in 1827, and reported so enthusiastically on the potential of the country that eager settlers took up all the suitable land in thirteen years. Those who followed had to look for runs further north, in the country opened up by Leichhardt, Dalrymple, and the young Jardine Brothers. As they settled in the area, coastal townships were established to serve them and became entry points for further settlers. So, within twenty-five years of the removal of the ban on free settlement, the squatters had performed the amazing feat of conquering almost the whole of Queensland.

Queensland's first governor, Sir George Bowen, described the squatter community as containing "a strong sprinkling of retired officers of the Army and Navy, sick of the routine of a Mess Room or Ward Room, of Oxford and Cambridge, men preferring an adventurous life in the open air to the indoor labours of a profession, and of other gentlemen of birth and education recently arrived from England." They had many problems and hardships. Good breeding stock was costly, and labour was scarce. Even those with pastoral experience gained in the southern States found it difficult to adapt their husbandry to tropical conditions, and lost many stock from feeding problems and human error.

The Aborigines, resenting their intrusion into tribal hunting grounds, retaliated by spearing men, horses, sheep, and cattle. In the 1860s, it was estimated that ten to fifteen per cent of the outback shepherds and stockmen were murdered, and guerrilla warfare between settlers and natives went on until the police got the situation under control in the 1880s.

Aboriginal spears were abetted by spear-grass, which infested the pastures and deteriorated the condition of the livestock. Dingoes mauled them and cattle-duffers stole them, and many of those that survived human and natural marauders perished on the long overland droving trips to market. Even so, the flocks and herds increased so rapidly that beef cattle grew from 1 million head in 1870 to 6 million in the 1890s. On the coastal plains, which proved to be unsuitable for sheep, these were replaced by cattle. The sheep were dispersed inland, and over a century have grown into the largest flocks in the world's tropical regions.

After an enthusiastic beginning, the infant pastoral industry collapsed under the weight of its own problems and debts. Abandoned properties glutted the market until they were revived by new developments. The local demand for meat, which had been negligible to start with, grew rapidly in proportion to the swelling populations of the mining towns. Boiling-down works transformed the surplus stock into hides,

King Ranch Cattle,
Tully.

tallow, and other by-products; more easily exportable than cattle on the hoof or the meat itself, which in those pre-refrigeration days would not stay fresh for more than a day or so. Meat prices soared, the industry rapidly revived, and was given a further fillip by the export of first canned and then frozen meat to Britain. Now, the pastoral industry is firmly established in tropical Queensland, and the original British breeds have been strengthened by virile exotic stock such as Brahman cattle. Large scale developments flourish. The King Ranch has carved a huge property out of virgin scrub outside Tully, and produce their famous tropically-oriented Santa Gertrudis beef cattle in large numbers.

Tropical Queensland is no stranger to exotic imports, and a memorial to some of these are the "Joss Houses," as Chinese temples were called with cheerful contempt. Remains of Joss Houses can be found in Atherton and Cairns, and the appointments of Cooktown's vanished temple can be seen in the museum. The best example is at Innisfail, and is open for inspection. The original served the Chinese community for nearly forty years, until its destruction in the 1918 cyclone,

"The Squatter"
(from "Picturesque
Atlas of
Australasia")

Chinese Temple
INNISFAIL

but it was rebuilt that year and used until 1940, when the
property was sold and the present Joss House built with the
proceeds. The garish interior, with its gongs, gilt, and images
of Buddha, is a window into the life of an almost vanished
community. Thousands of Chinese were imported to labour
on the goldfields, but few were able to bring their wives with
them. Labour contractors in China paid their passages to
Australia, maintained their families at home, and held back
a large slice of their earnings. About all that they carried with
them were their recreations and religion. As well as the Joss
Houses, opium dens, pak-ah-pu parlours, sly grog shops and
continuous gambling houses sprang up in the townships with
large Chinese communities. Pungent, colourful, and notori-
ous, these Chinese quarters attracted ladies of easy virtue and
the roistering sailors who pursued them.

But most of the Chinese spent years of patient toil in the
mines and on their market gardens, and then returned to
die in their ancestral villages. Not many of their descendants
remain, apart from those respected merchants and citizens
whose forebears chose to end their days in Australia.

UP THE REEF TO COOKTOWN

Ten miles south of Innisfail, and a few miles inland from beautiful Mission Beach and Bingil Bay, picturesque Mena Creek plunges fifty feet into a pool surrounded by lush rain forest, palms, and flowering shrubs. On the brink of the cascade is perched a baroque, grey-turreted castle; surprising and incongruous in the tropical setting. Known as Paronella Park, it was built by Jose Paronella, a determined Spanish migrant who carved sixteen cane plantations from the virgin scrub, sold them, and returned home to find a bride who would share his retirement on an estate of his dreams. He found the bride, but could not find any estate to match the beauty of his adopted land. So he returned to Innisfail in 1929, selected twelve acres of dense jungle surrounding Mena Creek waterfall and began slaving day and night to make his dream come true.

The simple, unlettered man, who knew little of architecture or landscape gardening, devoted twenty years to his Herculean task, and when he died his widow continued with

Paronella Park

Sugar Pioneer's
Monument, INNISFAIL

the work. She died in 1967, and since then their only son Joe
and his family have continued to make Paronella Park one
of the show places of North Queensland.

Power is generated by its own hydroelectric system, built
in 1933 and believed to be the first in Queensland.

On the bank of the Johnstone River at Innisfail stands a
life-sized statue of a cane cutter in heroic pose, to mark the
spot where Thomas Fitzgerald landed in 1880 to plant the
first stick of sugarcane. It was donated by the local Italian
community as a gesture to their adopted country.

Northwards up Highway One from Innisfail lies Cairns,
settled in 1876 and named after Governor Sir William
Wellington Cairns. In the 1880s, the outlook for Cairns was
bleak, but it was saved by the sugar farms spreading over the
fertile river flats and also by the first commercial banana
plantations. These were just being established in land cleared

from the scrub around the coastal settlements, and their quick cash crops attracted so many Chinese ex-miners that an enormous industry developed. But it declined almost as fast as it had grown. Even though the Cairns area alone produced a record crop of 38 million bunches of bananas in 1898, a large proportion of the unrefrigerated cargoes rotted en route to southern markets. The Tweed River district, which is considerably closer to Sydney, soon stole the bulk of · the trade, and the industry still flourishes in that area.

Cairns Harbour

During this century, Cairns has left bananas behind and
become one of North Queensland's five major sugar ports
and a thriving tourist centre. The countryside round about
offers splendid scenic contrasts, with the great mountain
ranges rising behind the lush sugar farms and sending cas-
cades tumbling down into the dense green rainforests.

If you enter Cairns from the south you see a wooded hill
which dominates the suburbs, and perched atop of it is the
historic "House on the Hill," a huge old homestead sur-

Pawpaws

Coconuts

Pineapples

Bananas

166

rounded by about ten acres of tropical vegetation. It was built by Richard Ash Kingsford, the first mayor of Cairns, whose daughter married a local banker named Smith. The couple joined their names together, too, and called themselves Kingsford-Smith, a name which became famous when their fourth son, Charles, who spent his childhood in the house, became one of Australia's most famous aviators.

During the second World War, the House on the Hill was requisitioned as headquarters for the combined Allied Commando Units and experimental station for the elite "Z" Special Units. Its isolation was so complete that few Cairns people knew what was being planned up on the hill. Amongst the secret and daring operations which were initiated in the old house was the successful sea raid on Japanese shipping by the disguised fishing vessel, *Krait*.

The present owners are developing the property into a tourist resort, and without destroying its original character the house has been converted into a motel and reception rooms which enjoy magnificent views of Cairns, Trinity Bay, and the mountains.

"The House on the Hill",
CAIRNS

The varied landscapes of the Atherton Tablelands, to the west of Cairns, are easy to reach by road or rail. Two deep crater lakes, Eacham and Barrine, lie in the heart of the Tablelands, surrounded by thick jungles which are reserved as National Parks. Kuranda, near the dramatic Barron Falls, has one of the world's most attractive railway stations.

Edmund Kennedy, as leader of an expedition to Cape York, was the first white man to penetrate the terrible scrub country of the coastal ranges, and in 1848 was speared by Aborigines as he struggled towards the coast in the hope of reaching the relief ship sent to succour his men. Most of his journal was lost, but subsequent reports by Hann and Mulligan attracted the first graziers and miners into the area. They were followed by timber-getters seeking cedar and other fine cabinet timbers.

When the best trees had gone, Chinese ex-miners carved out so many farms in the rich highlands that by 1900 they almost monopolised Tablelands farming. About 300 Chinese farms, mostly growing maize, were in the Atherton area alone,

Logging Mill

Hotel Fitzpatrick, Kuranda

but many of their small holdings were consolidated and extended when white settlers found that the Tablelands were ideal for dairy farming. Now, fresh milk from the rich pastures is sent on some of the longest milkruns in the world, as far as Mount Isa and Townsville.

Cairns is one of the jumping-off points for visitors to the Barrier Reef, the longest coral formation in the world. Over an estimated 30 million years, tiny calcium-secreting coral polyps have built a world of fantastic variety and beauty, and the colourful coral gardens and warm surrounding waters are home for myriads of sea creatures ranging from fish of many shapes and hues to bêche-de-mer, turtles, sharks, whales, and dugong.

The reef stretches from the Swain Reef, 150 miles to seaward of Mackay, for 1,200 miles up the Queensland coast

Barron Falls

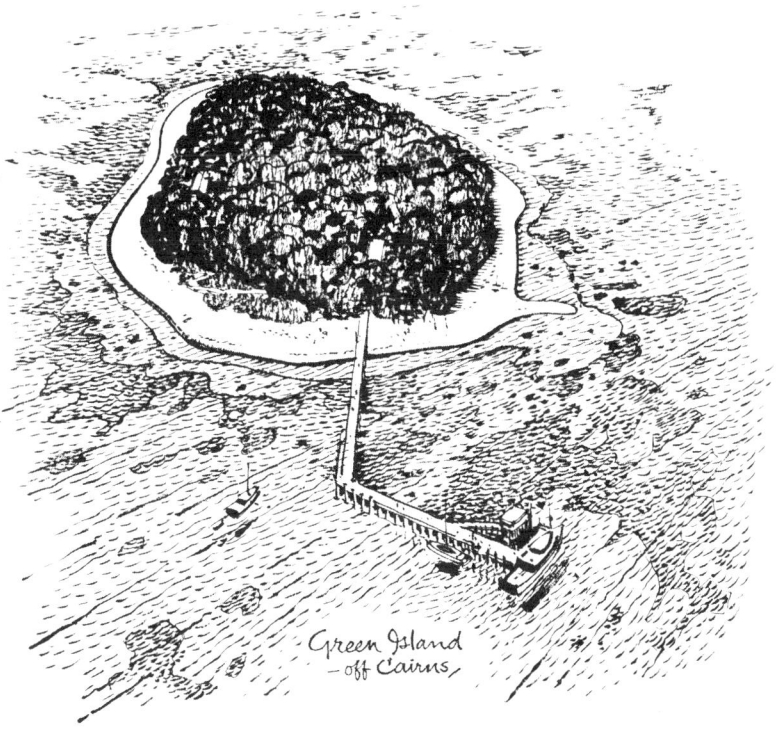

Green Island
— off Cairns

and through the Coral Sea almost as far as Papua. Scores of
beautiful islands lie between the mainland and the reef, but
the sea lanes between them contain many hazards known to
mariners since their charting by James Cook, Matthew
Flinders, and Phillip Parker King. The islands attract more
and more tourists from many parts of the world, who arrive
on the twenty island resorts by launch, light aircraft, or heli-
copter. More resorts are planned, to accommodate the
increasing influx of holiday-makers to this lovely area which
offers warmth and sunshine when the southern States are
locked in winter.

But the reef, which is one of Australia's most precious
natural heritages, is in grave danger. The Crown of Thorns
starfish, which feeds on living coral, has reached plague
proportions and caused widespread damage. Offshore oil
drilling, and chemicals washed down mainland rivers,
impose further threats which have caused alarm and protest.

"Crown of thorns" Starfish

Scientists from many nations have studied the Reef, and it will now be the subject of intense research by the Department of Marine Biology of the James Cook University of North Queensland. It is to be hoped that some of the problems can be solved.

Inland from Cairns, at Mareeba and Dimbulah, is the centre of Queensland tobacco growing, whose history holds as much "boom-and-bust" as that of the goldfields. But unlike Queensland cotton growing, which faded to nothing after a brief success when the American Civil War cut off Confederate cotton supplies to the English mills, tobacco has survived and flourishes.

The first three acres of tobacco were planted at Rockhampton in 1860, followed by experimental plantings on the rich flats of the lower Herbert River in 1874. These proved so successful that they foreshadowed Queensland's present important industry, but tobacco-growing continued as little more than a sideline until 1929. In that year, a Select Committee of Inquiry recommended the establishment of tobacco farms in Mareeba and Dimbulah, and there was a "tobacco rush" to the large areas of land thrown open for selection. Australian-grown tobacco was given the benefit of a lesser tariff than that which had to be paid on imported leaf, but in 1932 this was revoked and hundreds of farmers were ruined. They abandoned their properties, and Mareeba sank into a depression from which it did not emerge until it became a garrison town in the second World War.

After the war, the government settled ex-servicemen on irrigated tobacco farms along the Lower Burdekin River, and in 1948 a co-operative processing factory, with the largest tobacco display floors in the southern hemisphere, was built at Mareeba. Ten years later, Queensland's largest irrigation dam was built on the Tinaroo Falls. It took five years to reach its maximum storage capacity for water, which was channelled to the light sandy soil of the local tobacco farms. From a nucleus of successful farmers, many of them of Italian extraction who had remained there since Depression days, the industry grew strongly. Leaf from a

Tobacco,
Mareeba.

Walsh River farm reached the world record price, and Mareeba is now the thriving centre of closely-settled tobacco farms. They stretch for miles, with their rich green fields punctuated by the quaint silhouettes of the oast-houses in which the leaf is cured.

The present location of Mareeba was selected by John Atherton, after whom the Tablelands are named. He was attracted by the good grazing land described by that ubiquitous explorer James Venture Mulligan, and set out from the Burdekin with his family, 100 horses, and 1,500 cattle to become the Tablelands' pioneer pastoralist. Skirting the town site that now bears his name, he followed Mulligan's route northwards and built his shingle-roofed slab-hut overlooking the turbulent Barron River, where Mareeba now stands.

The age-old lure of finding an Eldorado had played its part in the development of North Queensland, and each new goldfield brought swarms of eager miners and those who battened upon them into the remote and inhospitable country. Even though so many failed, they had at least broken the trail, but the irony lies in the fact that they had eyes for nothing but gold. Some prospectors reported the presence of baser metals, but the enormous potential of these has only recently been realised.

Atherton, though primarily a cattleman, was bushman enough to recognise such minerals when he saw them. While

anthills

Old Herberton

seeking cattle in the Barron Valley, he and a companion panned alluvial tin in a creek he named Tinaroo. Later, he found more, where Mulligan had reported its presence on the Wild River, one of the headwaters of the Herbert. He told William Jack and his son-in-law, John Newell, who were interested in mining, and they were so excited that Newell rode 100 miles through uninhabited country to file his claim at Thornborough. The tin rush began, and new towns were born as the Great Northern mine on the upper Herbert, and John Moffatt's Irvinebank workings, yielded their riches to the nomadic miners. Jack and Newell carted in the provisions to supply them, and on the proceeds founded a chain of general stores.

The tin mines also attracted Chinese from the expiring goldfields. Some of them had experience gained on Malaysian tin workings, and made money wherever a show of metal could be found. Others turned to mining the copper discovered at Mount Garnet, Mount Molloy, and Chillagoe,

Port Douglas Beach

but as prices fell and Cloncurry and Mount Isa became major copper producers the fortunes of North Queensland copper declined. The mines were abandoned, and the once thriving communities were added to the ghost towns which crumble throughout the North.

One which survived is Port Douglas, though visitors to this serene port boasting "the best beach in the world" find it hard to believe that the rich mineral strikes on the Tablelands and the goldfields on the Hodgkinson once made it rival Cairns for the trade to the mining camps.

The forty miles of magnificent coastal highway between Cairns and Port Douglas must be one of Australia's most scenic drives. Settlement along the route began in 1877, after that solitary bushman and explorer Christy Palmerston had blazed a trail from the Hodgkinson River to Island Point. Though longer than the existing route from the Tablelands to Cairns, his track had a grade which could be negotiated by teamsters and mule packers, and even by the Cobb & Co coaches which began running in 1882.

Port Douglas
from the Nautilus

Old Mine / Court House Hotel
PORT DOUGLAS

In its 1880s heyday, Port Douglas had an estimated floating population of 36,000, who in that thirsty climate spent their earnings freely at the thirty-six local hotels. So much Port Douglas land was held by speculators in 1881 that they contributed to the revival of Cairns, because those who sought land during the sugar boom could buy it more cheaply at Cairns. Landowners who tried cattle-raising were defeated by Aborigines hungry for fresh meat, so they leased their land to the Chinese for rice-planting. The climate was right, but the market was small, and even a subsidy could not keep the industry alive. A promised railway connection did not eventuate, the expected golden future faded like so many others, and the little port fell into a sleepy decline from which it has been re-awakened by the tourist trade. Now, a solitary surviving hotel, some motels, and two fine restaurants cater for those who holiday in glorious surroundings.

A ruder awakening came briefly on 16 March 1911, when Port Douglas, Mossman, and Mount Molloy suffered badly in the cyclone of that year. One of the worst on record, it cut a huge swathe of destruction which wrecked the timber churches of the three townships, so the Council of the Parish of St David, Mossman, determined to rebuild in stone. The versatile Reverend Edward Taffs designed a church with a simple Byzantine character, and even laid much of the masonry of local fieldstone after the foundations had been laid in 1915. Committee followed committee, plans were made and changed, but the Reverend Taffs continued doggedly building until his death in 1950. He built the walls, with their natural rough texture accented by coloured quoin and gable blocks, to roof level, and his successor raised the money to complete nave and chancel. Transepts and vestries must be built by future generations. The charming little church, set amongst tropical trees, was consecrated by the Bishop of Carpentaria in 1952.

Lieutenant Cook, who sailed past the Port Douglas district in 1770, had no occasion to name any of its features until his ship the *Endeavour* grounded on a reef further north. He

Mossman Church

careened her in the estuary of the river which now bears the ship's name, and a century later the government was forced into hurried development of the Endeavour River as a seaport for men and stores pouring through it to the Palmer River diggings. Gold had been found there by Surveyor Frederick Warner, one of the party of a giant bushman, William Hann, on a Government-sponsored exploration of the Cape York Peninsula. Hann rewarded Warner with half-a-pound of tobacco, and it was left to James Venture Mulligan to follow up the lead. A veteran prospector and explorer, who did more than any other man to open up the vast mineral deposits of the Cairns hinterland and the Cape country, he confirmed that the upper Palmer held the richest alluvial gold yet discovered in the North but warned of the harshness of the almost inaccessible country. Gold-hungry diggers ignored him as they rushed the most spectacular but shortest-lived Queensland goldfield. It inspired "The Old Palmer Song," written in 1873, and wherever miners gathered they sang:

So blow ye winds, heigh-ho!
A-Digging we will go
I'll stay no more down
South, my boys
So let the music play.
In spite of what I'm told
I'm off to search for gold
And make a push for that new rush
A thousand miles away

"Panning-out"

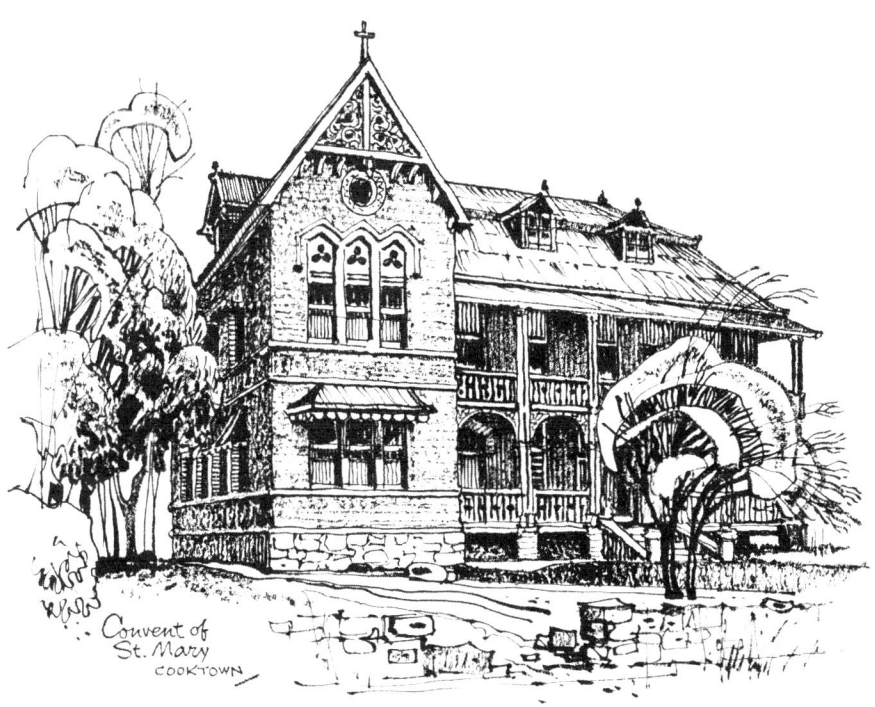

Convent of
St. Mary
COOKTOWN

"In spite of what I'm told" may have included stories of
the fearful axe-hewn track from Cooktown to the Palmer;
160 miles through choking jungle in which the fierce Aborigines of the area lurked. Even rougher was the shorter Hell's
Gate Track, over the Great Dividing Range. Hundreds of
Australians and Chinese died from disease, starvation, or
Aboriginal spears, but thousands more got through and sent
the gold pouring back into Cooktown. Within three years,
15,000 whites and 20,000 Chinese had passed through Cooktown on their way to the River of Gold, and they dug over
the goldfields to the tune of fifty-five tons of gold—plus
unrecorded amounts of smuggled metal. The gold went
quickly, the cost of living was astronomical and living
conditions bestial, so within a few years the river was
abandoned to patient Chinese fossickers. At last even these
drifted away into farm labour, or returned to China.

the 1803
Cannon
COOKTOWN

To most travellers, Cooktown is the end of their northern
journey, and it is hard for them to realise that the sleepy
township was once Australia's largest city north of the Tropic
of Capricorn. Pioneered by bêche-de-mer fishermen and
cedar cutters, it leapt into importance when it became the
port and trading centre for the sprawling goldfields of the
Cape, with a population during the 1870s of about 45,000
Australians, Chinese, and Kanakas. Now, its permanent
population is only about 450.

Ships from all over the world loaded gold, tin, pearl shell,
cedar and sandalwood in the broad Endeavour River
estuary. Three joss houses, thirty-three grog shops, and
various brothels and gambling dens served the coolies,
sailors, and diggers. The Chinese shanty town covered two
square miles, and often was a battlefield between white and
yellow miners.

Cooktown's "one day of the year" is the Queen's Birthday,
when a solemn group of townsfolk dressed in period costume
re-enact the landing of Lieutenant Cook and his crew. He
stayed for six weeks to repair the *Endeavour* after her ground-
ing on a reef off Cape Tribulation in June 1770, and not long
ago the six cannon jettisoned in order to float her off the reef
were discovered by American marine scientists. The once
derelict Convent of Saint Mary has been acquired and
restored by the National Trust and is now the Captain James
Cook Museum. The town has a fascinating collection

Monument to
Captain Cook

of relics from old Chinatown, the mining days, and Cook's voyages. One, much photographed by visitors, is an old cannon bearing the sign: "Cooktown Town Council on 10.4.1885 carried the following motion asking the Premier of Queensland that Cooktown be defended against the threat of a Russian invasion: — 'A wire be sent to the Premier requesting him to supply arms, ammunition, and a competent officer to take charge of same, as the Town is entirely unprotected.' This gun, cast in Carron, Scotl., in 1803, and two rifles were sent."

Cooktown has been re-discovered by the holidaymakers who find it rich in beauty and interest, and by the farmers who have found that every tropical crop will thrive along the Endeavour River flats.

North of Cooktown, Cape Flattery is marked by vast sandhills boldly sculptured by the trade winds. The three uninhabited islands of the Lizard Group, standing around a deep and lovely lagoon, lie about twenty miles north east of the Cape. They were visited in 1770 by Cook, who from their highest peak saw the channel winding through the maze of the Barrier Reef and named it Cook's Passage.

In 1881, the largest island had a population of five; Mary Watson, her fisherman husband and infant son, and their two Chinese servants. Before her marriage, Cornish-born Mary Watson had been a governess in Cooktown.

On 27 September 1881, while her husband was seeking bêche-de-mer on the reef, their hut was attacked by a band

Lizard Island Group

of Aborigines from the mainland. One of the servants was killed and the other wounded before Mrs Watson scared off the tribesmen with shots from her husband's rifle. But they did not go far, so she decided to escape. With her son and the injured servant, Ah Sam, she pushed out to sea in an iron tank, hoping to drift to the mainland or into sight of a ship. But they were swept onto a reef, where they stayed, hoping for rescue, until their water ran out and the undaunted Mrs Watson knew she must push on. She paddled the tank as far as one of the waterless islands of the Horwick Group, where all three died of thirst. Her pathetic little diary, recording their last days, is in the Cooktown Museum, and the tank is in the Queensland Museum. Now, Lizard Island may become a resort for big-game fishermen who will fish the edge of the Barrier Reef and the deep waters of the Coral Sea.

The remnants of Mary Watson's hut are being preserved on the island, so will not vanish completely as have so many other buildings of the past. Some which do remain are examples of the way in which early settlers modified traditional designs to suit their strange new environment. The founders of the northern cities had no local building tradition to follow, so they imitated the homes and public buildings of New South Wales, developed by military men on colonial service and the occasional convict architect such as Francis Greenway. They retained the symmetry and fine Georgian detail of the Colonial Style, and when this was adapted for the north a compromise with the tropical climate produced the deeply recessed windows and verandahs screened with lattice panels or cast-iron lacework. When major civic and commercial buildings were required, the architects were commissioned from the southern capitals and used much the same designs as those they had built from in their home towns.

Bush carpenters and migrant tradesmen were equally conservative, but gradually a distinctive home pattern evolved, much better suited to the climate and perhaps owing something to the bungalows of India and Malaya seen by settlers who had worked in those areas. In the 1880s, a visiting Canadian journalist was impressed by the stilted houses surrounded by deep verandahs, and also reported that "the banks and public buildings of Townsville are built in refreshing white, with colonnades and arcades, looking like places for human beings in a hot climate and not like gaols for lost spirits."

The early administrators must have had limitless faith in the future of the North, because they commissioned buildings which far exceeded their needs. One such is Townsville's fine Customs House, built in 1902 on the Strand, in a commanding position which overlooks shipping movements in the Harbour. To stimulate local industry the bricks and roofing tiles were made in Townsville. The granite facings were quarried on Magnetic Island, and the internal joinery

Customs House,
TOWNSVILLE

and appointments fashioned from northern cedar and silky
oak. Now it stands like a proud memorial to the days of
soaring optimism and drawn-out disappointments, on the
waterfront of the busy seaport which is living evidence that
Tropical Queensland has at last justified early medical
research and its founders' faith in its future.

DARLING DOWNS

Drawings by
KEVIN JOPSON

Text by
PETER NEWELL

CONTENTS

ALLAN CUNNINGHAM

Allan Cunningham discovered the Darling Downs on 5 June 1827. While searching for an alternative route to the Moreton Bay settlement, he crossed the Great Dividing Range through what is now known as "Cunningham's Gap" and descended into "a beautiful and well-watered valley, affording abundance of the richest pasturage and bounded on each side by a bold, elevated range."

Cunningham, who was born at Wimbledon, England, on 13 July 1791, was a complex man. At first he studied law, but his great love of plant-life inspired him to become a botanist. It was a love that possessed him for the rest of his life.

In 1816 he arrived at Sydney, after spending two years in Brazil. He brought several South American plants which he thought could be acclimatised in Australia. Soon he eagerly joined Oxley's expedition to search for fresh pastures for the Colony's rapidly expanding sheep flocks, then gained further experience when he served as botanist on Phillip Parker King's voyages along the northern coast of Australia. His account of King's survey was widely read, and was later translated into German.

However, the discovery of the Darling Downs was undoubtedly Cunningham's finest achievement. After returning to Sydney from the Downs, he tried to encourage settlers to select their runs on the seven million acres of rich country, but despite his enthusiasm it was twelve years before the Leslies took up the challenge in 1840. Eighteen months later settlers claimed an area as large as Scotland.

Cunningham died on 27 June 1839, two weeks before his forty-eighth birthday. He is remembered as a dedicated scientist and a resourceful man of action.

Cunningham's Memorial — Cunningham's Gap

STANTHORPE

While travelling along the border of New England, Patrick Leslie left his billy by a creek. He marked the campsite on his map with the words "Quart Pot," and the name stuck. By the 1850s Quart Pot Creek had become a regular stopping place for teamsters bringing supplies from Tenterfield and Warwick to the large pastoral stations in the area. A single-roomed bark inn was built near the creek.

Quart Pot's future prosperity was first glimpsed by a visiting police magistrate. He noticed that the stones in bags stacked as a wind-break around the inn were those of an ore-bearing rock, similar to that found in the New England tin mining district. In February 1872, two prospectors discovered rich tin deposits on nearby Maryland Station. Soon a thriving

Jopson

Granite C

township sprang up to serve the hundreds of miners who flooded into the area.

The Catholic Church decided to make Quart Pot the centre of a new diocese. However, even though the thirsty miners justified the town's name, the Church felt that the title "Bishop of Quart Pot" would be most unsuitable. The Government Surveyor aptly renamed the town Stannum, which later became Stanthorpe. In the following years a considerable quantity of tin, scheelite, and wolfram was mined. Some mining companies imported Chinese coolies to reduce labour costs, despite opposition from local miners.

When the alluvial tin was worked out, Stanthorpe was saved from becoming another deserted ghost town by the extension of the railway from Warwick in the 1880s. This enabled the unemployed miners to become orchardists within easy reach of markets, because fruit and vegetables grew well in the fertile Granite Belt. After the first World War returned soldiers were repatriated to the orchards, and their battle-fields are remembered in the names of nearby townships. Today, Stanthorpe is an important fruit growing district.

nthorpe

WARWICK

North of New England the highway winds through orchards and vineyards between the rugged hills of the Granite Belt, then enters the great plainlands dotted with famous stud farms. Patrick Leslie chose the site for Warwick on the banks of the Condamine River. Proclaimed a town in 1861, it soon became the centre of Queensland's first pastoral settlement.

Warwick's broad streets, memorial-studded parklands, and fine public buildings reflect the character of the district's pioneers. These wealthy pastoralists were technically trespassers, for they squatted on the best grazing country before the government released it for selection in 1842. Henry Stuart Russell, who had taken up Cecil Plains Station, graphically described the rush of new settlers as "dusty squatting-fevered tribes pursuing each other to the Downs . . . jostling each other as if the broad bush were not road wide enough; whip-cracking; oath-snapping; joke-cracking; smoke-sucking — on!"

"Leichhardt's Tree" stands near the entrance to the historic Rosenthal sheep station, and marks the outskirts of Warwick. It is said that the tree marks the spot where Ludwig Leichhardt set out on his ill-fated expedition in 1848. He was never seen again.

The district is heir to one of Australia's richest architectural heritages, the early builders having excellent local materials. Alexander Mayes and John McCulloch, two local contractors, built the dignified Warwick churches and public buildings. Allora, and the villages nestling between the mountain spurs, contain buildings that delight all admirers of the Australian Colonial tradition.

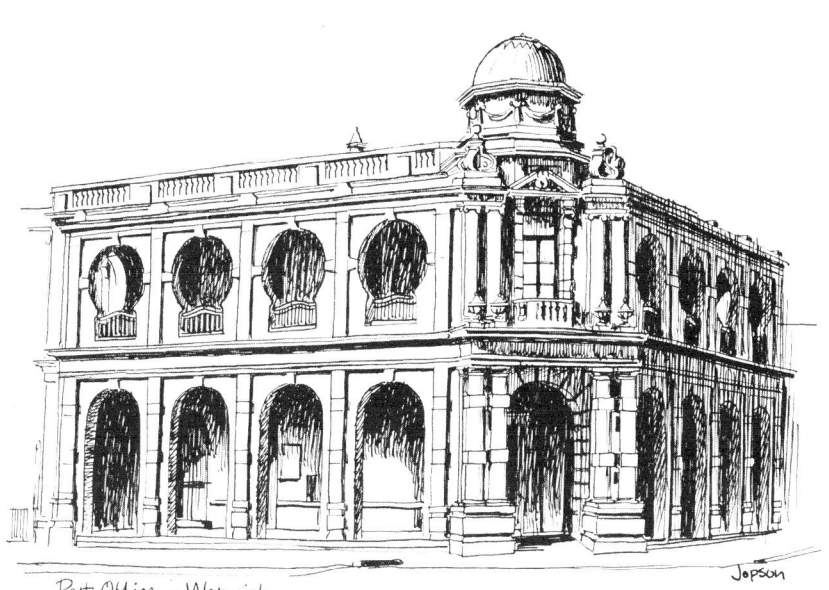

Post Office — Warwick

Jopson

Pringle Cottage — Warwick

Jopson

THE SCHOOLS

Many settlers on the Downs were from wealthy families, and they considered that a private tutor for their children was as important as their household cook. However, the Reverend Benjamin Glennie realised that there was an urgent need to provide schools for the children of smallholders and townfolk. After the separation of Queensland from New South Wales, he established an elementary school. At first lessons were held under a tarpaulin, but later a two-roomed slab hut was built beside the Dalrymple Creek at Allora. The teacher's family occupied one room, and the other was used as a classroom during the week and a church on Sundays. Earlier the Leslie family had sponsored a New South Wales National School at Warwick. It still stands in Fitzroy Street, proudly bearing the date 1850.

The first public school in the Toowoomba district was opened at Drayton on All Fools Day 1860. Here the settlers' children received basic education at the cost of one shilling per week. On 5 August 1875, the foundation stone was laid for the Toowoomba Grammar School, which was built on fifty acres of parkland partially donated by the government.

Several gracious old homesteads on the Downs were converted into boarding schools. The Slade family bequeathed Glengallon to the Church of England for their famous Slade School at Warwick. Tyson Manor formed the original Downlands College, and Kerrielaw now houses part of Ursuline Convent. Arranmore on the banks of the Condamine River near Warwick was acquired in 1919 for the co-educational Scots College.

A century after the original thirty-one pupils began classes at the Drayton school, the numbers enrolled at the many Darling Downs schools had multiplied a thousandfold. To provide tertiary education an Institute of Technology has been established at Toowoomba.

Toowoomba Grammar School — Toowoomba

Jopson

CANNING DOWNS, WARWICK

Patrick Leslie, the first settler on the Darling Downs, was born in 1815, the son of a Scottish laird. In 1835 he emigrated to New South Wales and proceeded to Macarthur's Camden property to study Australian pastoral methods. Shortly afterwards he met Allan Cunningham and was impressed by his enthusiastic description of the virgin country in the "Northern Districts." Accompanied by an assigned convict named Peter Murphy, he set out along Cunningham's marked tree line on 2 March 1840. They explored the country along the Condamine River, and Leslie selected the site for a head station which he called Canning Downs. A month later his brother Walter and twenty-one ticket-of-leave men reached the Downs after overlanding 5,700 sheep.

Jopson

The Leslies' first dwelling was a typical pioneer's split slab and bark roofed cottage, which Walter Leslie described as little better than a hen-coop. Five years later the brothers built a larger house in readiness for George Leslie's wife. The original house still serves as a detached kitchen wing.

When the homestead was added in 1854 by the Leslies' cousin, Gilbert Davidson, he faced the principal rooms eastwards to take advantage of the magnificent panorama of the Macpherson Ranges rising beyond the lush Condamine River Plains.

Canning Downs was chosen by the government as the site for an experiment in acclimatising South American llamas. It was hoped that a local mohair industry could be developed, but the mountain-bred creatures soon perished.

The city of Warwick covers part of the original Canning Downs station. Now the area of the once immense property has been drastically reduced, but the present owners, the Honourable and Mrs C. E. Barnes, still maintain a proud tradition with a well-known thoroughbred horse stud and cattle breeding.

y "Canning Downs" Homestead – Canning Downs

THE RISDON STUD

In 1842 a large tract of George and Patrick Leslie's vast squattage was granted to the Aberdeen based North British Australasian Pastoral Company, and was named Rosenthal. However, twenty years later this station was thrown open for closer settlement.

A Canning Downs employee named Crane selected part of the run and named it Risdon. At first he and his bride lived in a slab and bark shepherd's hut until he gathered enough raw materials to build a more substantial home. Waterworn stones for the walls and clay suitable for making sandstock bricks came from the nearby creek. Ironbark was cut into roof framing and rifted into shingles. The remains of a simple kiln where limestone was burnt for the mortar and plaster can still be seen on the bank of the creek.

Risdon has had six owners during its century of colourful history. Its fame spread when it was acquired by the Australian subsidiary of the huge King Ranch of America, and buyers from every State attended the first sale of their Santa Gertrudis cattle on 14 November 1952.

When Princess Alexandra represented the Royal Family during Queensland's Centenary celebrations in 1959, she spent a typically Australian country holiday at Risdon. The property was later bought by Mr Keith Leahy who concentrated on breeding thoroughbred horses.

The Crane's cottage formed the kitchen wing of the large two-storeyed homestead, but one night in 1968 a spark from the chimney ignited the graceful vines which had spread over the facade. After the blaze, only the original fieldstone walls were standing. As a link with the past, these walls were restored and integrated in the stud office and buyers' den of the new homestead.

Original "Risdon" Homestead — Warwick

NORTH TOOLBURRA

North Toolburra lies some eight miles north-west of Warwick. The name of the first lessee of this historic station has been much disputed, but it is now generally accepted that both North and South Toolburra were part of the Leslie brothers' original selection. However, it seems that they were unable to adequately stock the entire run, so they were forced to release large sections to the eager selectors who followed close on their heels. As a result, other famous stations such as Glengallon, Rosenthal, Goomburra, Maryvale, and Talgai were created in the Warwick district.

In 1852, North Toolburra was taken over by a pastoralist named Hood in partnership with John Douglas, onetime Premier of Queensland. It was managed by the versatile James Morgan, who later acquired his own property. He was a man with many abilities. Trained as a surveyor in Wales, Morgan served as the Mayor and Member of Parliament for Warwick, and also owned the local paper, which developed into the present *Warwick Daily News*. His son, Sir Arthur Morgan, became Premier and Lieutenant-Governor of Queensland. Morgan Park in Warwick is named after this distinguished family.

North Toolburra's third owners, Massie and Walker, used bricks baked on the property to build the fine homestead in 1859. It is now the home of Mr John Warner, a member of a well-known Downs grazing family.

The station has had several owners, although the Swinburne family, who acquired it from Thomas Coutts in 1895, held it for thirty-three years. Other owners have included the Earl of Suffolk and Berkshire, and the great-grandfather of Sir William Gunn, the former Chairman of the Australian Wool Board.

Woolshed "South Toolburra" — Warwick

TALGAI AND THE SKULL

Talgai, near Allora, was selected in 1840 by George Clark. He soon established a most successful merino stud, and in 1867 he commissioned an English architect named R. G. Suter to build him an imposing homestead.

The homestead is enormous by present standards, comprising three wings surrounding a courtyard. Yet documents discovered by the present owner, Douglas Panton, among the surviving station records, reveal that the original contract was for £2,000. A century later, the cost of building such a homestead could be conservatively estimated at 100 times that amount.

Internally, the exposed sandstone walls have recently been restored and redecorated, but the mellow rough-textured

"Talgai" Homestead

stone of the deep perimeter verandahs has been preserved in its original condition.

In 1886, William Naish and his two sons contracted to complete the fencing of Talgai's paddocks, but the torrential rains that ended the disastrous Australia-wide drought of the 1880s interrupted their work. When they returned, they found an unusual human cranium which had been washed out by floodwaters. The now famous "Talgai Skull" was displayed on a mantelpiece in the homestead for the next forty years, but its great scientific importance was not realised until it came to the notice of Professor Sir Edgeworth David in 1914. Recently Professor N. W. G. Macintosh of Sydney University relocated the place where the skull was originally discovered. He carbon-dated the shell and bone fragments found in the excavations, and as a result it is now believed that the first man came to Australia between 20,000 and 30,000 years ago.

"Talgai" is also remembered as the location of one of Queensland's first, although shortlived, goldmines.

Jopson

THE PURE MERINOS AND BEEF BARONS

We can thank Captain Philip Gidley King for our merinos. He persuaded Captain Waterhouse and Lieutenant Kent, the naval officers whom Governor Hunter had sent to South Africa to purchase cattle, to buy twenty-six sheep of the Spanish Merino strain. Thirteen survived the voyage to Sydney, where they were landed in 1797. They were sold to several landholders, including Captain John Macarthur, who crossed them with the sheep already in the colony.

The result was so striking that the pioneer pastoralists became enamoured with the merino breed in general, and during the 1820s they were imported from Saxony and Silesia. Special studs were established to improve the breed for local conditions. The oldest stud in Queensland was at Welltown, near Goondiwindi, where Studmaster Fred ("The German") Bracker made a major contribution to high grade wool production in the district by introducing 200 pedigreed Saxon merinos. His son continued his splendid work.

As the Downs was settled, the name "Pure Merinos" took on a new meaning. It was the term scornfully applied by the struggling farmers to the graziers of wealth and social distinction who, after taking up the best country, strongly resisted closer settlement. The privileged squatters' fine homesteads such as those at Cecil Plains, Jimbour, and Talgai, with their outbuildings, chapels, post offices, and schools, made some of their properties almost self-contained.

Oscar de Satge of Old Gowrie smugly described his fellow graziers as "leaving little to be desired in the way of reputation for industry, honesty of purpose and absolute good faith . . . What can a country desire more in the founders of her early history?"

Old Store and Quarters — Jimbour

Jopson

Old Customs House — Goondiwindi

Jopson

WOOL AND JACKIE HOWE

The Leslie brothers drove their original mob of sheep up to their Downs squattage with some trepidation because it was widely prophesied that the heat of the "Northern Districts" would turn wool into hair. Fortunately the sheep demonstrated their adaptability by doubling their numbers by 1843.

Sheep flocks on the Downs multiplied so rapidly that by the time of Separation (from New South Wales) in 1859 there were 1,500,000 grazing on the rolling grasslands along the Condamine River. The continuing expansion of the sheep population was astonishing because of the enormous losses due to drought, fire, flood, and disease. Moreover, they had to compete with kangaroos and rabbits for their feed, and prior to the protection of dog-fencing they were easy prey for dingoes and wild dogs. It was not until 1870 that wire fencing began to replace shepherds and folds made with wooden hurdles.

In 1854, Le Rosière's circus pitched its tents in Warwick. Its star performer was a famous acrobat named Jack Howe, who married the recently widowed companion of Mrs Patrick Leslie. Their son, Jackie, grew into a powerfully built man, with legs which measured twenty-six inches around the thigh and seventeen and a half inches around the calf. He was taught shearing by a Chinese on Killarney Downs, and soon became Australia's champion shearer. His 1892 world record of 321 sheep shorn in seven hours forty minutes with hand blades has never been surpassed. Indeed, it was not until the 1950 season that it was exceeded with a machine-driven handpiece. Jackie's son proudly perpetuated his father's record by naming his Dalby property "321."

Jackie used to cut off the sleeves of his shirts so that his movements were not restricted. His mates did likewise, and to this day these sleeveless woollen garments are known as "Jackie Howes."

Jopson

"THE APOSTLE OF THE DOWNS"

The Reverend Benjamin Glennie, who became known as "The Apostle of the Downs," was one of the Downs' most respected pioneers. He was born at Dulwich, England, in 1812, and studied theology at Christ College, Cambridge. Soon after his migration to Australia in 1848, he was ordained by the Bishop of Newcastle, who appointed him to the Moreton Bay parish, then the northern extremity of his vast diocese. Within a year Deacon Glennie had opened the Downs' first Anglican Church at the crossroads village of Drayton.

This dedicated clergyman and his old black horse became a familiar sight throughout the Downs. His long journeys to celebrate the squatters' marriages and baptisms took him as far west as the Condamine and Dogwood Creek districts. For shorter journeys he preferred to walk. It is recorded that in 1861 he walked from Warwick to Brisbane to meet an astonished curate who had just arrived from England. Then he escorted him back to his new parish, again on foot.

Although there were disputes with Aborigines in those days, the Reverend Glennie was never attacked when passing through tribal territories. This great churchman spent nearly thirty years of devoted service to the pioneer families scattered throughout the Downs. During his ministry at Warwick he established new churches and the first schools in the infant settlements.

Reverend Glennie finally retired to Brisbane where he died at the age of eighty-eight. He is remembered by the Glennie Memorial School for Girls at Toowoomba and Glennie Heights overlooking Warwick, where his sandstone residence is now the cherished home of Mr and Mrs H. A. Leonard.

Church of England — Drayton

Church of England — Leyburn

213

TOOWOOMBA

The first resident of Toowoomba was Josiah Dent, a station hand who set up his tent at "The Swamp," which was then the eastern extremity of Westbrook Station. His lonely task was to gather bulrushes in the insect-ridden marsh. Meanwhile, the early settlers at "The Springs," now Drayton, were considering the potential fertility of this waste country if it could be drained. They managed to reclaim land for twelve twenty-acre farms out of the swamplands. These were soon cultivated because they were within easy reach of the Toll Bar route to the Moreton Bay settlement.

At first, Toowoomba consisted only of a few rough timber buildings which had developed around the small farming community. The farms were rather resented by the local squatters, who regarded them as misuse of good pasturage. In 1855 a turnpike was erected on the Toll Bar, and twelve years later the railway was built from Ipswich to Toowoomba. By 1876 the steady development of the Downs made it necessary to extend the railway to Dalby.

Toowoomba developed accordingly, but although it is now entering its second century as Queensland's largest inland city, its Town Plan still reserves four-fifths of the land for rural areas. The altitude of the Range allows English trees to flourish in the many fine parks, giving a distinctive character to what must surely be one of Australia's most gracious provincial towns.

Today Toowoomba is not only the commercial and industrial hub of the Downs, but has become an important educational centre and provides all the facilities for its citizens to enjoy a full cultural life. It is the home of well-known Australian writers and artists, the annual festivals attract a growing number of tourists, and dedicated gardeners hold a Carnival of Flowers each spring.

"Clifford House" — Toowoomba

"Vacy" — Toowoomba

THE GERMAN SETTLERS

When North Queensland's rich goldfields were discovered, farm and station hands deserted their jobs and joined the rush to the new El Dorado. Consequently the colony was faced with a severe labour shortage.

The German Consul in Sydney realised that his compatriots fleeing from religious persecution would make good settlers, and he directed the first German migrants to the Darling Downs in 1854. Further German settlement was stimulated by Johann Christian Heussler, a Brisbane merchant who made several trips to his homeland to encourage rural workers and artisans to migrate.

Before leaving Germany, each migrant signed a contract binding him to work for a minimum of two years as a shepherd or boundary rider. Their annual wages were only £30 to £40 plus rations and quarters, but many saved enough to establish their own farms.

Other ships followed, bringing German girls to marry the single farmers. Soon women with baskets of produce on their heads for barter or sale became a common sight in the Toowoomba township. Within ten years, 11,000 Germans had accepted the challenge and had been welcomed by the government with assistance and gifts of land in districts reserved for closer settlement.

The Premier, Sir Thomas McIlwraith, enthusiastically reported in the Legislative Assembly: "Coming from the boat the Germans appear in their national garbs, they are seen a day or two in the depot, then all at once they disappear into the bush. Nothing is heard or seen of these people anymore till about 18 months or 2 years later; then they appear again. But how? Driving his own carriage, drawn by well-groomed horses, the German, with his wife and child, comes to town. They are well dressed, and upon their faces is seen the spirit of contentment."

Lutheran Church— Aubigny

'Jopson

THE FARMERS

"The Darling Downs will not grow a cabbage!" scoffed John Watts, the Member of Parliament for the Western Downs in 1860. He was typical of the "Pure Merino" squatters who selfishly fought to restrict closer settlement farming. However, the gently undulating plains soon demonstrated their fertility by growing a wide variety of cash crops. Indeed, an American agriculturalist visiting Dalby made another oft-quoted remark when he said that, "If we had such rich soil back home, we'd bag it and sell it as fertiliser."

Viewed from the air, the thousands of farms extend to the horizon like a vast, colourful patchwork quilt. It is hard to realise that Allan Cunningham waged a twelve-year battle to encourage settlement of this country, now recognised as one of the richest agricultural areas in the world. Although comprising only one-eighth of Queensland, the Downs produce one-tenth of Australia's wheat and one-third of its sorghum, as well as substantial quantities of other grains, dairy produce, meat, and cotton.

The rich soils, up to thirty feet deep in some areas, are the result of decay of volcanic rock over millions of years. As the plateau bounded by the Great Dividing Range falls away to the west, the red and chocolate loams of basaltic origin change to black clays rich in plant foods. The orchards of the Granite Belt thrive on the soils derived from the decomposition of the ancient granite spurs. Further west the black soil plains abruptly change to dry, sandy country.

Profitable farming was only achieved after years of perseverance, frustration, and unrewarded toil. Droughts and floods forced many despairing settlers to leave their farms, while others battled against high costs and low prices. At last the long struggle was won, and the rich farmlands on the Downs are a tribute to human courage and endurance.

Early Threshing Machine — Chinchilla

Oast Houses and Early Tractor — Inglewood

THE COTTON PLANTERS

The history of cotton growing on the Downs dates back to the American Civil War. When the Union States attempted to destroy the economy of the Confederate States by blockading the southern ports, the huge English cotton industry was cut off from raw materials and a depression settled over the mill towns. Thus the manufacturers were forced to search for other supplies.

Good quality Sea Island cotton had been successfully cultivated around Brisbane since the earliest days of settlement. Samples sent to England were eagerly accepted by the spinners, so the Queensland Government encouraged local cultivation by paying a bounty. Led by the enterprising Captain Robert Towns, the settlers cleared the river flats to

Cotton Gin and Bales — Cecil Plains

the west and south of Brisbane, and imported cheap Kanaka labourers to produce the profitable cash crop destined for the mills of Lancashire.

By 1866 the plantations had spread over the Range to the Downs, where 14,000 acres were put under cotton.

This thriving industry collapsed with the end of the Civil War. The American planters soon recaptured the English markets, the bounty was removed, and the booming export of raw cotton declined. The industry did not revive until fifty years later, when home consumption began to support limited dry cotton farming in Queensland.

In the early 1960s, two experimental farms in the Brookstead district showed that the yield of cotton per acre could be tripled by irrigation. Other farmers soon turned to cotton, under the guidance of government advisers. The local production is now sufficient to support two ginneries which have recently been established by the Cotton Marketing Board at Cecil Plains, and the future for this industry looks as bright as it did in the days of Abraham Lincoln.

STEELE RUDD AND THE SELECTION

At Drayton there is a memorial cairn marking the birthplace of the district's most celebrated character—Arthur Hoey Davis. He was born there in 1868, the eighth child in a Welsh blacksmith's family of thirteen children.

Davis wrote under the pen-name of Steele Rudd, and his stories have become part of our folk-lore. The inscription on the cairn reminds the traveller that "To Australian Life and Letters, he brought the rich gift of honest laughter—with undertones of the struggles and sorrows of the Pioneers."

After mining for tin unsuccessfully at Stanthorpe, his father took up virgin land at Emu Creek. His battle to wrest a farm out of the wilderness inspired his son's famous "Selection" books. From 1895, when the Sydney *Bulletin* published his short sketch entitled *Starting the Selection*, Rudd poured out a torrent of stories until his death in 1935. He recorded with sympathetic understanding the toil and heartbreak of the cocky farmers' lives.

Rudd led a full life. He attended the local school, then started work as a rouseabout on a nearby station, where he became an expert horseman. Later he was employed as a clerk in the Curator of Intestate Estates office in Brisbane. At the same time he reported on rowing, his favourite sport, for the local Press. In 1903, he resigned from the Public Service and devoted his life to writing his tales. They have recently been reprinted with the original Lindsay illustrations for the delight of yet another generation of Australians.

There are two memorials to the writer on the site of the Davis' shingle hut—a stone marker and a wooden pole on which the names of the family are carved. At the Drayton School, a "Steele Rudd Corner" contains a collection of items of interest about his life. His memory is also kept alive by an annual pilgrimage to his cairn.

ARTHUR HOEY DAVIS
"STEELE RUDD"
BORN NOVEMBER 14, 1868 DIED OCTOBER 11, 1935.

TO AUSTRALIAN LIFE AND LETTERS, HE BROUGHT THE
RICH GIFT OF HONEST LAUGHTER – WITH UNDERTONES OF
THE STRUGGLES AND SORROWS OF THE PIONEERS

INSCRIBED BY THE TOOWOOMBA LADIES LITERARY SOCIETY
THIS MEMORIAL WAS RAISED ON THE SITE OF THE AUTHORS
BIRTHPLACE BY THE PEOPLE OF AUSTRALIA

Steele Rudd Memorial – Drayton

Jopson

223

DRAYTON AND THE BULL'S HEAD

Drayton was one of the first villages on the Darling Downs. It grew up around an intersection of tracks where the bullock teams rested after their long haul up the Range. Soon a few merchants and a blacksmith started business in slab and bark roofed huts. This small settlement was known locally as "The Springs," but Thomas Alford, who had set up a trading post there in 1842, named it Drayton after his Somerset birthplace.

The first inn on the Downs was owned by William Horton, who is remembered as the founder of Toowoomba. New Drayton is part of Toowoomba's suburbs, but the Bull's Head Inn still overlooks the wagon trail, which has developed into the busy highway from the southern Downs. The original inn was the scene of many historic meetings, including the first Church of England Service, conducted by the Reverend Benjamin Glennie on 20 August 1848.

Ten years later, the small slab-sided building became inadequate for the growing community, so Horton built a new inn with seventeen rooms and four attics, as it stands today. It was constructed of local hardwoods, with joinery and furniture fashioned from the rich red cedars which were plentiful in the district.

When the licence expired in 1879, the inn was sold as a private home and post office to the Lynch family, who renamed it "The Terrace." The old weatherbeaten building is still owned by Mrs Lynch's son. It is such an important link with the pioneering days that it must be preserved for future generations.

Old "Bull's Head" Inn — Drayton

Jopson

225

CAST IRON LACEWORK

Much of the character of the early buildings on the Downs is derived from their delicate cast-iron tracery. Nowadays, most of the slim cast-iron posts which once supported shop awnings have been removed by municipal order. It is typical of the Australian disinterest in our architectural heritage that beautiful cast-ironwork, which is jealously preserved for tourism in New Orleans, is disappearing from our townscapes.

No material influenced late Victorian architecture more than cast-iron. Its popularity extended over fifty years, and it was cast in huge quantities by the English foundries. This versatile material was usually shipped to Australia and the southern states of America as ballast in the windjammers. It was so cheap to buy and fix that it was applied to buildings ranging from humble cottages to proud hotels and imposing mansions.

An insatiable demand developed for a material so attuned to an age of display, and soon Australian foundries commenced manufacture. Many of the geometric English patterns were protected by copyright, so the local manufacturers began competing with each other to produce coarser and more florid designs. They even turned to Australian wildlife for inspiration; koala bears, cockatoos, and lyrebirds abounded among fern fronds and gumnuts.

Cast-iron has been rediscovered by the present generation, and the demand has outstripped the supply from the demolition of old buildings. Therefore, a new source of lacework has been found. The original cast-iron nostalgically mimicked the elegant English handwrought iron of an earlier age. Now it is the turn of cast-iron to be mimicked by cast-aluminium, which gives a surface finish simulating many coats of paintwork damaged by the usage of the years.

Hotel at Allora

Jopson

Jopson

Original Council Chambers — Allora

WESTBROOK

John ("Tinker") Campbell is remembered as the first squatter in Queensland. When he emigrated from Maine, U.S.A., he brought a consignment of tinware which he hoped to trade with the Aborigines. However, hostile tribes near his cattle run on the McIntyre River forced him to follow the Leslie brothers to the Darling Downs. In 1841 he selected 110,000 acres of choice country which he named Westbrook.

"Tinker" Campbell held his huge acreage for only four years, then sold the property to Henry Hughes, from Worcestershire, for only £400. In the following years he earned another nickname: "Never-to-be-beaten". His activities ranged from curing beef for export and boiling down sheep for tallow to timber milling, coal mining, and operating a saltworks.

The next owners of Westbrook were John Donald McLean and William Beit, who acquired the remaining 80,000 acres. In 1867, they replaced the timber homestead with a sturdy bluestone house with two-feet thick walls, roofed with imported slates.

When the gold-rushes depleted the labour force, Chinese and Kanaka labourers were employed on the stations. But the Chinese soon moved on to the goldfields, and the unacclimatised Kanakas died of pneumonia.

Westbrook's acreage was considerably reduced in the 1870s when its "scrubby ridges" were cut into eighty acre farms for closer settlement.

The Couper family occupied Westbrook for some fifty-one years, after which it was purchased by the H. McPhie family, who renovated the homestead during their five years residence. This gracious building, which has played a significant part in the history of the Downs, is being further restored by the present owners, the Gifford family.

Westbrook Homestead — Westbrook

Jopson

OLD GOWRIE

Henry Hughes and Fred Isaac, two Worcestershire lads, decided to try their luck in Australia. However, they were soon disillusioned with their Hunter Valley farm, so when they heard Patrick Leslie's glowing account of the country in the "Northern Districts" they eagerly set out for the promised land.

After an eventful overlanding, during which they were held up by bushrangers, they squatted on lush plains land in 1841. Their run was bounded by the Range and the country selected by "Tinker" Campbell earlier that year. They called it Gowrie. Hughes and Isaac were technically trespassers, as it was not until 1842 that Governor Gipps decreed the area open for settlement.

"Old Gowrie" Homestead — Kingsthorpe

Their original holding covered 80,000 acres; the entrance gate was at the present intersection of Ruthven and Russell Streets in the heart of Toowoomba. Traces still remain of the kangaroo-proof paling fence that completely surrounded the property to save the pastures from the plentiful wildlife, the despair of early settlers.

In 1866, Colonel H. Venn King formed a partnership with Edmund St Jean and Oscar de Satge to acquire the lease. When he converted to freehold he bought out his partners and founded the firm of King and Sons. They operated a profitable colliery on the property in addition to their pastoral work.

The huge century-old homestead, which can be seen from the Western Highway, took seven years to build. It was constructed of fully imported materials, and the floor was built over a labyrinth of stores and cellars. Old Gowrie has recently been bought by Mr and Mrs W. J. Makim, who have commenced the formidable task of restoring this grand old Colonial house for another century of grace and charm.

JIMBOUR: DALBY

In 1841, Richard Todd Scougall was licensed to take up ground "beyond the limits of location." He selected a vast run extending from the Bunya Mountains to the Condamine River, and called it Jimbour, meaning "lush grass".

Two years later Scougall overlanded 11,000 sheep and 700 cattle from the Hunter Valley, but financial troubles forced him to sell Jimbour to Irish immigrant, Thomas Bell, and his three sons. The youngest son, Joshua Peter Bell, was only twenty-one, but he vigorously managed the selection, which had been reduced to 211,000 acres by the Commissioner of Crown Lands. Fire destroyed Scougall's original split slab cottage, so the Bell family replaced it with a house built of Toowoomba bluestone. The ground floor rooms still serve as staff quarters and stores at the rear of the present imposing mansion built in 1874. F. D. G. Stanley, the Colonial Architect, used local stone and red cedars hauled from the Bunya Mountains. Only the Welsh roofing slates were imported.

The Bell family showed remarkable enterprise in supplying services for the property. Artesian bore-water was pumped into a water tower by Queensland's first windmill. Gas for lighting was generated from coal mined on the station.

J. P. Bell became Sir Joshua Bell, with a high reputation in the public and commercial life of Queensland. But a run of low prices and bad seasons, culminating in the slump of the 1890s, forced the Bell family to assign Jimbour to the banks.

After Wilfred Adams Russell acquired the property in 1923, he began the task of restoring the neglected homestead. More than 1,000 guests attended a banquet to mark the re-opening of Jimbour House on 21 November 1925. It is now the home of Charles Russell. Jimbour is the pride of the district which owes so much to the Bell and Russell families.

"Jimbour" Homestead — Jimbour

233

THE BUNYA MOUNTAINS AND JIM CROW

The eastern rim of the Downs is bounded by the escarpments of the Main Range, which extends northwards in a gentle curve from the abrupt peaks and valleys that surround Cunningham's and Spicer's Gaps, finally terminating in the Bunya Mountains. From the Dreamtime, the Darambal and Waka Waka people hunted the plentiful game on the rolling plains, but every third autumn the ripening of the nuts in the huge Bunya pine cones heralded the time for their migration to the mountains. There they were joined by tribes from surrounding districts for their feast of the Bunya nuts, an occasion for corroborees and celebrations.

When the lumbering of pines and cedars in the Bunya Mountains commenced, the hauliers chose an overnight resting place for their bullock teams near a large hollow tree. According to a folk tale, a wandering Aboriginal named Jimmy Crow lived in the tree. The name of Crows Nest, the farming district which has developed nearby, was derived from this story. In 1969, a memorial to mark Crows Nest's centenary was considered, and the committee decided to erect a statue of Jimmy Crow. They commissioned the versatile Fred Gardiner, a retired Downs grazier, champion axeman, and sculptor. Visitors to his Tia Art Gallery at Toowoomba were fascinated to watch him carving the life-size image out of a thirty-five hundred-weight block of Helidon freestone.

Unfortunately many fine stands of native timbers have gone from the Bunyas, but 27,950 acres of virgin rain forests covering the slopes have been declared a National Park.

"Jim Crow's Nest" Memorial — Crow's Nest

THE BANKS OF THE CONDAMINE

"Died by Act of Parliament, the township situated on the banks of the Condamine River. It sprang into existence about A.D. 1860 and lingered, a sickly institution, till All Fools Day 1879 when it passed quietly away."

An indignant storekeeper inserted this bitter obituary notice in the Roma newspaper, following the government's decision in 1879 to re-route the western railway through Miles, instead of Condamine.

The original settlement had developed around the junction of roads from the south and west where the river was easily fordable. Bullockies and horse teamsters rested there, and later it became a staging station on Cobb and Co.'s Dalby-Roma run. When trucks superseded wagons, the weary drivers of motor transports carrying goods and stock still pulled up at the pub on the banks of the Condamine.

The pioneer pastoralist Matthew Goggs held the first "roving licence" in the district, until the boundaries of his run were defined in 1848. A year later Richard Birrell took up 48,000 acres between the Condamine River and Dogwood, and named the station Tieryboo.

In the early days, bells to help locate stock straying over vast distances were scarce and expensive. However, in 1872 an ingenious local blacksmith named Jones fashioned bells out of old cross-cut saw blades, rivetted and brazed into a distinctive narrow-mouthed pattern. They were so successful that they could be heard up to seven miles away on a clear night. Jones and his assistant, Christy Andersen, supplied the demand for the "Condamine bells" for many years.

Early School — Pioneer Museum at Miles

Jopson

Condamine Bell

"Twickenham Cottage" — Miles

Jopson

237

THE PRICKLY PEAR STORY

A few miles from Chinchilla there is a modest building which bears the inscription "Boonarga Cactoblastis Memorial Hall". It was built by local graziers as a tribute to an unpleasant-looking insect named *Cactoblastis cactorum*. The pastoralists and farmers had every right to be thankful, for this South American moth has saved Queensland over $200,000,000.

At one time the dreaded prickly pear ruined millions of acres in New South Wales and Queensland. It was first introduced into Australia by Captain Arthur Phillip. While the First Fleet was provisioning in Brazil, he collected cochineal insects and their host plant, the prickly pear, to ensure a supply of dye for his soldiers' red coats. Some early Downs settlers innocently planted cuttings to provide ornamental stockproof hedges around their homesteads. The plant flourished and attracted fruit-eating birds, which spread the seeds throughout eastern Australia. Eventually the prickly pear was spreading at the rate of 2,000,000 acres a year, and some of it grew more than ten feet high. "Prickly pear pulpers" were used in an attempt to soften the spines and convert the pear into stock feed.

As properties were abandoned and stock starved to death in the thickets, the desperate government turned to the entomologists to find means of checking the infestation. In the 1920s "egg-sticks" of the Cactoblastis and other enemies of the prickly pear were imported from South America, and insect colonies were distributed throughout the worst affected areas.

The success of the scheme was miraculous. Within three years the ravaged pear country was made even more fertile by the mulching from the dead plants, and the pastoralists resettled an area greater than Tasmania.

Prickly Pear Pulper – Chinchilla

239